Kristopher L Williams

THE THEOLOGY OF FREEDOM

THE THEOLOGY OF FREEDOM

THE LEGACY OF JACQUES MARITAIN AND REINHOLD NIEBUHR

by
John W. Cooper

MERCER

ISBN 0-86554-172-8

Library of Congress Cataloging in Publication Data
Cooper, John W. (John Wesley), 1953–
    The theology of freedom.
    Bibliography: p. 177.
    Includes index.
    1. Christianity and politics—History—20th century.
2. Maritain, Jacques, 1882–1973—Contributions in
political science. 3. Niebuhr, 1892–1971—Contributions
in political science. I. Title.
BR115.P7C66   1985   261.7′092′2   85-13852
ISBN 0-86554-172-8

CONTENTS

PREFACE

Ours is the age of political theology. The contributions of Christian theology to our understanding of the political order have been immense. Today, the welter of divergent, and even contradictory, ideological positions is maddening. Yet, clarity amid confusion is possible. Christian political theology in the twentieth century has two great beacons of clarity—one a child of Rome, the other a child of the Reformation.

The Roman Catholic and Protestant styles of Christian political theology find paradigmatic expression in the writings of two prominent, twentieth-century theologians, Jacques Maritain and Reinhold Niebuhr. While each represents a distinct strand of the Christian tradition, they both arrived at a political viewpoint advocating democratic pluralism and respect for human rights. They both elaborated a theology of freedom. A comparison of their substantial writings on political theology reveals not only their essentially practical point of view, but also the distinct traditions and styles that shaped their thought.

The political theologies of Maritain and Niebuhr must be approached on their own terms. The key interpretative insight for Maritain is "practical wisdom"; for Niebuhr it is "realism." For Maritain, practical wisdom is closely related to the traditional Christian virtue of prudence. By comparison, Niebuhr understands realism in terms of the tension between the virtues of love and justice. Through the application of these basic insights, both Maritain and Niebuhr reveal the ambiguities of morality and power politics in the modern world. They survey the history and sources of Christian political theory and uncover unique contributions to the age-old discussion of what constitutes a just society. They outline the ideals and realities of contemporary democratic pluralist society with its fundamental orientation toward the protection of human rights.

Nevertheless, the several styles of Christian political theology remain distinct. There are many and diverse ways of understanding the relationship between the "two realms" of the sacred and the secular, the spiritual and the temporal. Maritain's thought is an example of an *analogic* relationship between the two realms; Niebuhr's thought epitomizes a *paradoxic* relationship. These two approaches, which must be examined in some detail, are complementary opposites. This validates the ironic but still valid observation that, for Maritain and Niebuhr, practical agreement emerged from divergent theoretical foundations. Such a provocative and profitable comparison of the political theologies of Maritain and Niebuhr—a Roman Catholic and a Protestant—suggests the possibility of finding in their work some common ground for an ecumenical, political theology based on support for democratic pluralism and human rights.

The subject of this study—the relationship between religion and politics as expressed in the writings of Jacques Maritain and Reinhold Niebuhr—should be of enduring interest to those with an eye for the workings of practical intellect. One finds in the works of these two eminent thinkers a philosophical depth and a practical sophistication that is truly rare. Furthermore, not only do they faithfully represent their respective traditions, Roman Catholicism and Protestantism, but they also speak to the universal community of persons.

It was with deep respect and admiration that I undertook this exposition and comparison of their ideas. I approached the data not only with the curiosity of a historian, but also with the hope of an ethicist who fervently seeks insights into the foundations of a genuinely ecumenical, social ethic for our time.

I wish to acknowledge my deep gratitude to the professors from whom I have learned to interpret and revere the primary texts of Christian political theology, especially Leo Sandon, Jr., John J. Carey, Richard L. Rubenstein, Michael Novak, D. B. Robertson, and James B. Wiggins. Each in his own way was a source of intellectual stimulation and personal encouragement; without them, this work would have been impossible. The value of this work is in large part due to their help; its shortcomings are entirely my own.

Portions of this essay have appeared in print as follows: "Jacques Maritain and Reinhold Niebuhr: Theorists of Democratic Pluralism," *Catholicism in Crisis* 1 (July 1983): 35-38; "Democratic Pluralism and Human Rights: The Political Theologies of Jacques Maritain and Reinhold Niebuhr," in *Jacques Maritain: Philosophe dans la cité*, ed. Jean-Louis Allard (Ottawa: Institut International Jacques Maritain, forthcoming).

I am grateful to the following persons and publishers for permission to quote from copyrighted materials: to Dr. Ursula Niebuhr for Reinhold Niebuhr's *Christian Realism and Political Problems, Man's Nature and His Communities,* "Thomism and Mysticism," and review of *True Humanism;* to Harper and Row Publishers, Inc. for Reinhold Niebuhr's *An Interpretation of Christian Ethics* and H. Richard Niebuhr's *Christ and Culture;* to *Union Seminary Quarterly Review* for Reinhold Niebuhr's "Bergson and Maritain"; to The University of Chicago Press for Jacques Maritain's *Man and the State;* to George Braziller for Reinhold Niebuhr's *Faith and Politics;* to Holt, Rinehart and Winston for Jacques Maritain's *The Peasant of the Garonne;* and to Charles Scribner's Sons for Jacques Maritain's *Freedom in the Modern World* (1936), *Integral Humanism* (1968), *Reflections on America* (1958), *The Rights of Man and Natural Law* (1943), *The Social and Political Philosophy of Jacques Maritain* (1955); and Reinhold Niebuhr's *The Children of Light and the Children of Darkness* (1944), *The Nature of Destiny of Man* (1941), *Reinhold Niebuhr on Politics* (1960), and *The Structure of Nations and Empires* (1959).

Political Theology
in Perspective

A realist conception of human nature should be made the servant of an ethic of progressive justice and should not be made into a bastion of conservatism, particularly a conservatism which defends unjust privileges.

Reinhold Niebuhr
Man's Nature and His Communities[1]

---

[1]Subtitled *Essays on the Dynamics and Enigmas of Man's Personal and Social Existence* (New York: Charles Scribner's Sons, 1965) 24-25.

I

The political writings of Jacques Maritain (1882-1973) and Reinhold Niebuhr (1892-1971) are focused upon a rather specific concern within the fields of philosophy and theology generally. The focus is "political theology." At the most basic level, this term designates the intersection of politics and religion—or, more precisely, of political philosophy and theology. It implies, therefore, the search for a social and political vision with an essentially theological base. All theology, including political theology, necessarily includes a view of God, a view of the world and history, and a view of man—both individual man and collective man. Therefore, not every political vision can claim a theological base, nor claim to be a political theology.

What is Christian political theology? How are politics and religion to be understood? Are conflicts between political obligations and religious obligations inevitable? These are some of the questions that Maritain and Niebuhr tried to answer; and they are questions that still concern Christians today.

In the history of Christian thought, the idea of political theology has been commonly referred to as the problem of the Kingdom of God or the problem of the two realms. The "Kingdom of

God" signifies the historical and transhistorical goal of the Christian life; the idea of "two realms" raises the issue of the proper relationship between the spiritual and the temporal, between the absolute and the relative, or between the Kingdom of God and the whole multitude of kingdoms or regimes in human history.

"Political theology" is a term that has had two opposing meanings in the history of Christian thought, especially in recent times.[2] On the one hand, "political theology," as in the German expression *politische Theologie,* has been used to imply that political realities properly belong to the divine and sacred order. Thus the object of political theology is not secular and temporal but holy, making the historical realization of a "Sacred Empire" both possible and desirable. On the other hand, "political theology," as in the French expression *théologie politique,* can have an opposite meaning. In this view, political realities are understood as belonging to the secular and temporal order. However, because they concern morality and human destiny, they must be judged in the light of spiritual values, which have their source in the divine and sacred order. Thus, the object of political theology is not holy but secular and relative; no historically realizable regime deserves the name "Sacred Empire." Politics is a proper subject of reflection for the theologian because human relationships and social institutions are shaped by moral values, by spiritual values, and by first principles regarding God, man, the world, and history.

Maritain clearly rejects the former sense of political theology, which envisions the establishment of a "Sacred Empire." He notes that Carl Schmitt and other theologians of the Nazi era had "tried to show in the major political and juridical ideas of modern times a transposition of essentially theological themes." The Nazi theoreticians had pronounced a holy blessing on totalitarian policies. In our time, the effort to give theological justification to particular political movements is an alluring temptation. Nonetheless, for

---

[2]I am indebted to Jacques Maritain for this distinction. See his *Integral Humanism: Temporal and Spiritual Problems of a New Christendom,* trans. Joseph W. Evans (New York: Charles Scribner's Sons, 1968; rpt., Notre Dame IN: University of Notre Dame Press, 1973) 99-100.

Maritain, "there is a political theology as well as a political philosophy—a science of an object *secular and temporal,* which judges and knows this object in the light of revealed principles."[3]

For Niebuhr, as well as for Maritain, it is an error to sacralize any temporal regime or empire. Part of the uniqueness of Western Christendom, according to Niebuhr, lies in its doctrine of the two realms and its understanding of "the difference between the historical and the divine." To confuse the temporal order with the divine is to invite unspeakable injustices. Niebuhr considers entirely justified those criticisms of "religious politics, which identify the historical with the divine." No temporal city can be equated with divine perfection. For a civilization to do so would be to make "the perennial religious mistake of identifying its political idealism and will to power . . . with its god, or source of ultimate meaning."[4] In his monumental work, *The Structure of Nations and Empires,* Niebuhr showed how pervasive this false type of political theology has been in the history of both Western and Eastern empires.

The writings of Maritain and Niebuhr reveal an understanding of political theology that judges all temporal regimes from a permanently critical, but also responsible, point of view—a political theology that properly distinguishes between the "two realms" and comprehends the relationship and ultimate unity of the earthly and heavenly cities. This conception of the meaning and role of a critical-responsible political theology is theoretically applicable within any society or culture. Any nation can be based upon a clear distinction between sacred and temporal reality; and any people can imagine a system with relative autonomy between religious and political authorities. Yet in actual practice, many, if not most, nations of past and present history have tended to see themselves as "Sacred Empires," and have sought to create

---

[3]Ibid., 100.

[4]Reinhold Niebuhr, *The Structure of Nations and Empires: A Study of the Recurring Patterns and Problems of the Political Order in Relation to the Unique Problems of the Nuclear Age* (New York: Charles Scribner's Sons, 1959; rpt., Fairfield NJ: Augustus M. Kelley, 1977) 122.

unitary, religiopolitical regimes. This is true where Christianity is the substance of culture, and it is also true where other religions prevail. This partly explains why so much uncritical nationalism abounds, and why awful violations of basic human rights are committed in the name of "Sacred Empires." Nevertheless, in a world of emergent probabilities,[5] it will always be possible, as Maritain and Niebuhr suggest, to create a political society based on religious insights and theological values without, at the same time, claiming for it a sacred and absolute legitimacy.

Maritain, Niebuhr, and the Western Heritage

The dimensions of Christian political theology can be traced in detail by examining the work of these two twentieth-century theologians.[6] Jacques Maritain was a French Roman Catholic philosopher, a metaphysician, who elaborated a political theory based on the philosophical vision of Thomas Aquinas. He became one of the preeminent spokesmen for democratic pluralism and human rights in the contemporary era. Reinhold Niebuhr was a German-American Protestant pastor and seminary professor of social ethics whose voluminous writings on political issues were infused with a distinctly moral and theological viewpoint. He became the primary representative of the "realist" school of American political philosophy. Maritain and Niebuhr came from divergent backgrounds and must be understood as intellectuals standing firmly within mainstream Roman Catholicism and Protestantism, respectively.

They both relied on a wide range of sources available in the history of Christian political theory, including biblical, classical,

---

[5]On the concept of emergent probability as a solution to the problem of historical freedom versus determinism, see Bernard J. F. Lonergan, *Insight: A Study of Human Understanding*, rev. students' ed. (London: Longmans, Green & Co., 1958; rpt., New York: Harper & Row, 1978) esp. 121-39.

[6]I take the liberty of calling both thinkers "theologians." In fact, Jacques Maritain refers to himself as a Christian philosopher "sufficiently versed in theology" to concern himself with such matters. See his *The Peasant of the Garonne: An Old Layman Questions Himself about the Present Time*, trans. Michael Cuddihy and Elizabeth Hughes (New York: Holt, Rinehart & Winston, 1968; rpt., New York: Macmillan Co., 1969) 192.

Jewish, Roman Catholic, Protestant, and secular sources. By blending the ideas and insights of the entire Western cultural tradition, they succeeded, together and separately, in constructing a viable ecumenical social ethic for our time. Insofar as a cohesive vision of political theology emerges from their work, it is possible to speak of it as a typically "Christian" social vision.

A capsule statement of Christian political theology and its relevance to the modern situation is not easily found. What is the essence of the just society? Maritain and Niebuhr each devoted lifelong energy to the exploration of this problem. Their admirers remember them for their realistic views of the dual human capacity for justice and injustice, and for their commitment to a progressive political ethic. A capsule expression, which is in tune with the political theologies of both men, is "democratic pluralism and human rights," or simply "freedom," in the political sense of that term. In this study, I will be using the latter as a shorthand expression for the former.

Two other brief expressions of the nature of the just society can be found in the most enduring aphorism from each man's teachings. In the case of both Niebuhr and Maritain, the most remembered quotation is also one of the most representative and all-encompassing. Reinhold Niebuhr wrote, "Man's capacity for justice makes democracy possible; but man's inclination to injustice makes democracy necessary."[7] Jacques Maritain wrote, "The state is for man, not man for the state."[8] Not only do these statements reveal a fundamental consistency and complementarity, but also they reflect a spirit that is essentially biblical and Christian. Man is capable of good and evil; he is also called to create a political society of mutuality and love.

What is the biblical view of political man? Maritain and Niebuhr both may have thought of the famous passage in which Paul

---

[7]Reinhold Niebuhr, *The Children of Light and the Children of Darkness: A Vindication of Democracy and a Critique of Its Traditional Defense* (New York: Charles Scribner's Sons, Scribner Library, 1944) xiii.

[8]Jacques Maritain, *Man and the State* (Chicago: The University of Chicago Press, Phoenix Books, 1951), epigraph on the cover of this 1951 paperback edition.

discusses "the governing authorities." Outside of the Gospels themselves, there is probably no more profound and poetic expression of the just society than the brief discourse on the governing authorities in the thirteenth chapter of Paul's letter to the Romans. One must remember, of course, that in a democratic society the "authorities" are, ultimately, all persons.

> Let every soul be subject to the governing authorities. . . . Render therefore to all their dues . . . respect where respect is due, and honor where honor is due. Owe no man anything, but to love one another. . . . Love never wrongs a neighbor, therefore love is the fulfillment of the law. . . . Let us walk as in the day . . . not in strife and envying (Rom. 13:1-13).[9]

A second biblical passage that has been of crucial significance for Christian political theology is, "Render therefore to Caesar the things that are Caesar's, and to God the things that are God's" (Matt. 22:21). In fact, Maritain comments extensively on this saying in one of his earliest books on political theology, *The Things That Are Not Caesar's*.[10] This command of Jesus is a general statement expressing the need to distinguish the two realms of political and spiritual life and authority, but it is so general as to allow a variety of interpretations. In fact, Jesus' command to render to Caesar and to God is the foundation for several distinct types of Christian political theory. Clearly, though, the biblical view of man sets forth both a worldly responsibility and a supernatural calling. Without both aspects, no theology can claim the name "Christian."

Maritain and Niebuhr place the biblical view of man and his role in the political order at the heart of their political theologies. They endeavored to set out their political theories in keeping with the biblical norms of prudence, justice, and love. Yet they also understood that the traditions of the church and of the broader

---

[9]The passage is freely paraphrased from several versions. For a discussion of Maritain's exegesis of this passage, see the section "Maritain and Niebuhr on Paul's 'Powers That Be' " in ch. 3.

[10]Jacques Maritain, *La Primauté du Spirituel* (Paris: Librairie Plon, 1927), which appeared as *The Things That Are Not Caesar's*, trans. J. F. Scanlan (New York: Charles Scribner's Sons, 1930).

Western civilization must contribute to any complete political theology.

What other sources of political theology did Maritain and Niebuhr appropriate to produce their vision of the just, pluralist society? Western Christianity is a tradition richly endowed with affective and conceptual distinctions between the sacred and the secular, between absolute and relative authority. According to Maritain and Niebuhr, the main components of this tradition include the biblical texts and the sensibilities and insights derived from Jewish, Roman Catholic, and Protestant sources. In addition, Christianity has assimilated and adapted to its God-centered vision many of the ideas of classical Greece and Rome, as well as those of modern, secular thought. Each of these sources rightly belongs to the patrimony of the contemporary free society.

The basic foundation of political theology is the belief that God is just—that justice is an unmistakable attribute of the divine. If God is God, if God is worthy of worship, then God must be the perfect expression of Truth and Goodness, an utterly righteous God; and this divine perfection must necessarily constitute something superior to every partial and imperfect reality. This is the essence of the biblical teaching that God will sit in judgment upon the world, rewarding the good and condemning the evil. The ancient Song of Moses is a beautiful hymn of praise to such a God: "The Rock, his work is perfect; for all his ways are justice. A God of faithfulness and without iniquity, just and right is he" (Deut. 32:4).

Niebuhr frequently refers to the ancient Hebrew concept of a righteous God as a key element in the development of a political ethic. The Bible testifies to the justice of God and calls on the people of God to strive to conform to this lofty standard, to act justly, and to seek to establish a just society. The Bible also reveals that the people of God will continually fail to establish perfect justice, until God's kingdom comes at the end of time.

The commandment to do justice is intimately connected with the biblical view of man. The human person is both created in the image of God and a sinful, fallen creature. Similarly, society—collective humanity—is both *imago Dei* and sinful at the same time. Maritain repeatedly emphasizes this paradox of human sinfulness and spiritual destiny. Humans are responsible both for the evil they commit and for answering the call to strive toward sinlessness through the grace of God.

Christian political theory, according to Niebuhr, owes a special debt to the tradition of Judaism, and especially to the Hebrew insights into civic virtue and social justice. In Judaism there is a profound awareness of the social nature of human existence and a strong drive toward just relations among persons. There are at least three specific sources for this Jewish component of political theology. First, there is the prophetic tradition of ancient Israel. The prophets of old spoke harsh words of condemnation for the sins against God and against mankind that were committed by the Hebrews and by other peoples. Second, there is the strong tradition of respect for law that has always been central to Judaism. Israel, along with other nations, was not considered exempt from the obligation to place unswerving faith in God and to conform to God's standards of justice. The law and the prophets belong to the essential core of Christian political theology. Finally, there is a sense of social justice in Judaism that derives from the Jews' long history as a minority, a diaspora among the nations. As a minority living among other peoples, Jews have been inclined to be critical of any established authority, especially when its power becomes oppressive.[11]

Maritain and Niebuhr both agree that the major Roman Catholic components of political theology are derived primarily from a "natural law" tradition that combines classical Greco-Roman notions of justice and equality with the Christian virtues of prudence, justice, and love. The two differ, however, in their assessments of the adequacy of a natural law approach to political theology. Roman Catholic natural law tradition, like Judaism, has emphasized the belief that man is a social creature whose destiny lies in a collective realization of spiritual and temporal abundance. The emphasis upon the common good of the whole com-

---

[11]The Jewish contributions to the idea of social justice are discussed in Reinhold Niebuhr, *Pious and Secular America* (New York: Charles Scribner's Sons, 1958; rpt., Fairfield NJ: Augustus M. Kelley, 1977) 91-95.

munity has led Roman Catholicism to be more universalistic in its outlook than the more individualistic interpretations of Christianity to which Protestantism tends. This universalism has generated a powerful concern for human rights and a particular passion for the well-being of oppressed minorities.

Maritain and Niebuhr both agree that the principal contributions of Protestantism to a broadly Christian political vision derive from the notion of the freedom of conscience. They differ, though, in their assessments of the final adequacy of freedom of conscience. Although always a part of biblical anthropology, the idea of individual conscience and responsibility was a special concern of the Protestant reformers. The freedom of the individual conscience before God and the notion of salvation as a voluntary, personal experience, laid the groundwork for modern conceptions of democratic self-government and civil liberty. If the individual possesses transcendent freedom over against the religious community, then similarly, every person has political rights that transcend the interests of the political community. Liberty thus emerged as an aspect of justice and as a treasure belonging not only to individuals for their own sake but also to the community itself for the sake of openness to fuller ethical development.

In addition to the various theological resources that have informed Christian political theory, Maritain and Niebuhr believed that many lessons have been learned in the historical experience of modern secular society. The great achievement of modern society was pluralism. Given the great diversity of ideas, traditions, and loyalties that Christians have inherited from their past, it followed that society would either impose a unitary vision at the expense of one part of the Christian family of faiths or it would choose a pluralistic organizational model. The violent clash of religious groups eventually gave way to the open society of religious pluralism. A diversity of faiths was tolerated within an overall Western milieu. It thus became possible to speak of "Western culture" and, somewhat imprecisely, of a "Judeo-Christian" heritage. Alongside religious and cultural pluralism, there arose a diversity in political life—with representative democracy as its vehicle—and a diversity in economic life. Each group or individual was free to defend its interests and pursue its goals as long as its activity did not infringe upon the rights of others. The modern secular society, at its best, became not a value-less and godless regime but a political society based on a pluralism of moral and spiritual values.

Maritain and Niebuhr made use of each of these diverse strands of Western cultural and religious tradition in their political theories. In the final analysis, both theologians constructed a progressive political ethic. That is to say, both saw in history a thrust toward the ever-increasing realization of human freedom and self-determination. Both constructed a forward-looking ethic of prudence, justice, and love. Likewise, both saw possibilities for greater realizations of human freedom and moral development in the future. But Maritain and Niebuhr were realistic progressives. They saw the need for institutional restraints on the will-to-power, greed, and envy of humanity. Together they produced a social and political ethic thorough enough and flexible enough to serve as an ecumenical common ground for all Christians today. Moreover, theirs is a political ideal that can be affirmed by all persons of good will, whether Christian or not, who share a concern for justice and order, freedom and human dignity.

Both Maritain and Niebuhr constructed a political theology of freedom, a theology based on democratic pluralism and human rights. In their mature years, both rejected the extremist positions on the left and the right of the political spectrum. They worked to foster an awareness of the depths of insight in the legacy of Christian political theology. Yet they were men of their age. They sought to rescue the germ of truth from every philosophy or movement that enthralled their contemporaries. They envisioned a thoroughly modern, yet thoroughly Christian, political ideal.

The Public Dialogue of Niebuhr and Maritain

Because they shared so many of the same concerns at the same time, one wishes that Niebuhr and Maritain had engaged in an ongoing conversation throughout their careers. Unfortunately, the interaction in print between Niebuhr and Maritain is largely limited to three books reviews written by Reinhold Niebuhr in the late

1930s and the early 1940s.[12] The three books in question are Maritain's *Freedom in the Modern World*, *True Humanism*, and *Ransoming the Time*. On the whole, these reviews by Niebuhr suggest deep intellectual affinities between the two theologians, yet they also point out some basic differences in their presuppositions.

Beyond these three book reviews, the printed dialogue between Maritain and Niebuhr is negligible. They made only passing references to one another's thought in their writings.[13] However, it is also true that a great deal of verbal interaction between Maritain and Niebuhr took place. During the many years in which Maritain lived and worked in North America, the two theologians frequently crossed paths. Raïssa and Jacques Maritain were occasional dinner guests of Ursula and Reinhold Niebuhr, and vice versa. Given the outgoing and intense personalities of these individuals, there was surely a substantial amount of serious conversation about common concerns and issues of the day.[14] Unfortunately, the content of these personal encounters is

---

[12]For the full text of the three reviews, see the Appendix.

[13]Niebuhr refers in print to Maritain's concept of natural law, which Niebuhr appears to understand as typical of the Roman Catholic thought during that era. Niebuhr argues that there is "a permanent structure of human personality," but that there are "always historically contingent elements in the situation which natural law theories tend falsely to incorporate into the general norm." (See *Faith and History: A Comparison of Christian and Modern Views of History* [New York: Charles Scribner's Sons, 1949] 180.) Maritain mentions Niebuhr in a letter to June Bingham, dated 9 May 1958, now on file in the Manuscript Division, Library of Congress, Washington, D.C. "It is a good idea," Maritain writes, "to write a life of Reinhold Niebuhr. I have much admiration for his person. From the point of view of theology there are many differences between him and me (he is Protestant, I am Catholic). That which I especially appreciate in him is his breadth of vision and the spirit of faith with which he approaches contemporary problems, especially social problems, and his profound sense of the responsibilities of the Christian in temporal matters" [author's translation].

[14]In an unpublished letter to D. B. Robertson, dated 25 March 1982, Ursula Niebuhr writes, "The Maritains certainly were good friends. We saw quite a lot of them. . . . Reinhold thought him perfectly delightful, but found him a little bound by his scholastic categories and also less vigorous and irreverent than, for example, Etienne Gilson. . . . [They] talked about politics a good deal, after all it was wartime and the fate of the world was in the balance. . . . [They] were very sympathetic and both of them obviously enjoyed talking to each other."

lost forever to those who would compare their ideas. We can assume, though, that these were very special occasions quickened by the clash of great minds and spirits, sometimes agreeing, sometimes differing, but always congenial.

Reinhold Niebuhr first reviewed a book by Jacques Maritain in 1936. His review, entitled "Thomism and Mysticism," treats two volumes, Maritain's *Freedom in the Modern World*, published the same year, and Nicholas Berdyaev's *Freedom and the Spirit*, published a year earlier.[15] Niebuhr draws no comparisons between the two volumes, treating each independently of the other, in spite of the similarity in titles. Niebuhr finds *Freedom in the Modern World* to be a useful attempt to solve the "cultural and social crisis" of Western civilization through a balanced and theistic brand of humanism. He notes that Maritain rightly criticizes "secular humanism," whether liberal or communitarian, as well as the "less humanistic theism" of Protestants like Karl Barth.

Avoiding these two dangerous extremes, Maritain "reveals the very great resources of a genuine theistic humanism, which most moderns have ignorantly spurned." This theistic humanism is preferable to the Barthian Protestants' derogation of the human for the sake of elevating the divine. And it is preferable to the two dominant forms of secular humanism, the capitalist and Communist systems. On the one hand, Maritain "is able to escape the individualism of secular liberalism with his emphasis that the good of the community is the highest value 'in the scale of terrestrial values.'" (Maritain's critique of individualism mirrors Niebuhr's Christian Marxian view of capitalist civilization). On the other hand, Maritain "avoids the final subordination of the individual to the community as an end in itself by his insistence that the ultimate possibilities of personality transcend the social purposes for which individuals are claimed in their various political and economic collectivities." Maritain's warning that the Communist path leads to the abuse of individual persons resembles the criticisms that Niebuhr himself had begun to level at his fellow Marxians. Maritain warns against the neglect or perversion of

---

[15]*Saturday Review*, 8 August 1936, 16.

genuinely humanistic values, and Niebuhr is in substantial agreement with him.

However, Niebuhr also levels some sharp criticisms at Maritain's "unconvincing" suggestions for practical policy. "Maritain is more successful in commending a Catholic theistic humanism as a basis for a new world culture than in working out the political and economic details." As Niebuhr shows, Maritain endorses neither the capitalist nor Communist model of society. In its place, Maritain seems to want "a type of guild socialism." Niebuhr finds this unrealistic. He argues that guild socialism's controls over labor and product markets are not effective methods of achieving justice in a highly technical civilization, advocating instead even greater political control over economic power. According to Niebuhr, Maritain "pleads for a priority of politics over economics but does not face the problem that a technical age has made economic power the most basic power, from which political power is derived." Niebuhr argues that Roman Catholic social teaching geared to agrarian societies will not solve the problems of technological societies.

Niebuhr finds an additional weakness in Maritain's theory of the relationship of church and state. Maritain becomes lost in "unconvincing ambiguities" when he tries to expound a church-state relation that avoids the extremes of secularized toleration and authoritarian theocracy. "He does not face the fact that every cultural and spiritual institution is in constant danger of becoming the handmaiden of the dominant forces in society," including the "economic interests." Niebuhr implies that he is sympathetic to Maritain's desire to avoid both the radical separation and the uncritical identification of church and state. But Niebuhr does not think the practical solutions that Maritain proposes—such as the refusal to form Catholic political parties in order to assure the presence of committed Catholic members in all parties—are clear enough. While Niebuhr can agree or sympathize with Maritain on several important aspects of his political theology—the value of theistic humanism, for example—he raises penetrating questions about the methods or policies that will further their common goals.

Niebuhr's second review of a book by Maritain appeared in 1939.[16] The book is Maritain's *True Humanism*, later retranslated under the title *Integral Humanism*. Again Niebuhr has high praise for Maritain's work: "one of the ablest analyses of the difference between Christian and modern humanist presuppositions which could be found." But again Niebuhr sees difficulty with Maritain's plan for constructing a future society that is truly just. Niebuhr wonders how the inherent authoritarian structure and disposition of the Roman Catholic Church and Roman Catholic principles can be reconciled with democracy. Nevertheless, Niebuhr finds many valuable insights in *True Humanism*. "Of all Catholic interpretations of modern ethical and religious problems, that of Maritain . . . would probably come closest to the views generally held by socialist Christians of Protestant persuasion," a description that Niebuhr intends to apply to himself. Maritain is "a profound Catholic philosopher with a genuine appreciation of the social problem."

Perhaps most significant of all, Niebuhr finds in Maritain a genuine political liberal who challenges the presuppositions and consequences of Marxism. One of the central themes in the intellectual journeys of both Maritain and Niebuhr was their encounter with Marxism. As young men they had both embraced the idealism and passion for social justice that they found in this new political philosophy. They enthusiastically joined the assault on a status quo that had become resigned to the existence of unjust privileges in society.

As a teenager, Maritain had written, "I will be a socialist and I will live for the revolution. . . . Everything I will think and know, I will consecrate to the proletariat and to humanity."[17] At that time, to be a socialist was to belong to the heroic French revolutionary tradition. Maritain would later, after his conversion to Roman Ca-

---

[16]Reinhold Niebuhr, Review of *True Humanism*, by Jacques Maritain, in *Radical Religion* 4 (Spring 1939): 45.

[17]Jacques Maritain, *Carnet de Notes* (Paris: Desclée de Brouwer, 1965) 16-17. This passage is translated and quoted in Joseph Amato, *Mounier and Maritain: A French Catholic Understanding of the Modern World* (University AL: University of Alabama Press, 1975) 30.

tholicism, become associated for a time with the rightist and antisocialist *Action Française*. Clearly, there were several divergent influences at work in the intellectual development of Maritain.

Likewise, Reinhold Niebuhr first entered the political fray during a time of bitter conflict between labor and management, socialists and capitalists. The birth of the auto industry in Detroit was the occasion for the emergence of "big labor" as a countervailing force to "big business." In 1933 Niebuhr stated, "Marxism gives the key to the real facts of capitalistic civilization."[18] Nonetheless, it is clear from his early writings that Niebuhr sought a self-critical Marxian theory and praxis. In the same writings in which he praises certain Marxist critiques of capitalism, he criticizes certain tendencies of both socialist and communist parties. Over the course of several decades, he maintained his belief that the economic power of the owners of the means of production must be placed in check by other centers of power. But he became increasingly critical of the Marxist myth of history, which assumed that the problem of justice could be easily solved by the concentration of political, economic, and moral-cultural power in the hands of a single elite. In his later writings he praised the emergence in the free societies of a pluralism of social forces that was gradually eliminating the unjust privileges of early capitalism.

In his mature years, Maritain also rejected Marxism, especially its atheistic and materialistic philosophical assumptions. Like Niebuhr, he recognized the success of the nominally capitalist nations in creating pluralistic societies that had achieved proximate justice through the mechanism of political checks and balances. Although Maritain was much less concerned with problems of economic justice than was Niebuhr, he too was encouraged by the development of what he called "economic humanism"—which today might be called "social market economy" or "democratic capitalism." Maritain noted the emergence of a new regime in which labor and management increasingly

---

[18]Reinhold Niebuhr, "A Reorientation of Radicalism," *The World Tomorrow* 16 (July 1933): 443-44.

tended to serve the common good of society.[19] He spoke of the need for a new understanding of economic justice that went beyond the old ideological division between "laissez-faire" and "revolution."

The encounter of both Maritain and Niebuhr with Marxism is a key element in the story of their contributions to contemporary Christian political theology. Marxism was in many ways a negative catalyst to the emerging Christian political theology of both men. While it was their ideological starting point, their later, refined writings traced the outlines of democratic pluralist society with its emphasis on the protection of human rights.

In fact, as early as 1939, in his review of Maritain's True Humanism, Niebuhr was able to rehearse the points of agreement between them:

> He is critical of Marxism at precisely the points where we have been critical. He sees that Marxist utopianism is a necessary consequence of its naturalism and materialism. It desires to establish the Kingdom of God in history and thus expects the unconditioned good within the relativities of history. But unlike most Catholic critics of Marxism, he has a genuine understanding of the fateful and necessary role which the workers must play in the reconstruction of society and of the genuine contributions which Marxist philosophy has made to their discovery of that role.[20]

Once again Niebuhr concludes that in Maritain he has found a Catholic philosopher whose thought is congenial with his own. He has found a true liberal, a true humanist, someone who is captive to neither the sentimentality and utopianism of the extreme left nor the cynicism and authoritarianism of the extreme right.

The final review by Niebuhr, entitled "Bergson and Maritain," gives notice to two books, Jacques Maritain's Ransoming the Time and Raïssa Maritain's We Have Been Friends Together.[21]

---

[19]Jacques Maritain, Reflections on America (New York: Charles Scribner's Sons, 1958; rpt., New York: Gordian Press, 1975) esp. ch. 13.

[20]Niebuhr, Review of True Humanism, 45.

[21]Union Seminary Quarterly Review 3 (March 1942): 28-29.

Niebuhr discovers that the one theme uniting both books is the philosophy of Henri Bergson. As a young couple, the Maritains had attended Bergson's lectures in which he stressed the "importance of history" in contrast to the "rationalism and relativism" of the dominant intellectual circles. Yet Bergson's philosophy, Jacques and Raïssa concluded, was but "a half-way house to Christianity." Niebuhr notes that while Bergson explains everything in terms of the experience of duration, Jacques Maritain "proves that duration is an inadequate category of ultimate reality, that life cannot be understood except from the standpoint of the divine reality which transcends the flux of time." Raïssa Maritain's book reveals the autobiographical side of this journey through Bergson's philosophy to Christian faith.

This discussion of the philosophy of history has serious implications for political theology. Indeed, Christianity does stress the importance of history, and it looks with approval upon human efforts to improve the social order and alleviate suffering. Nonetheless, Christianity does not worship history or progress. The world is fallen, and therefore history has only relative value. It exists in tension with, and in subjection to, a higher, transhistorical reality. Thus, Christian political theology is progressive without being utopian. For Maritain, as well as for Niebuhr, history is the arena of God's purposive activity and man's cocreative potentiality.

These three reviews reveal that Maritain and Niebuhr had different spiritual personalities, distinct presuppositions, and world views. Yet there was a deep affinity between their two systems of thought. The basis of their agreement was a common biblical view of human nature and destiny, informed by the wider patrimony of Western civilization. In addition, they also shared an appreciation for the institutions of a free society and the historical experiment of the Western nations in democratic pluralism and the defense of human rights. Their affinity suggests the potential for developing an ecumenical political ethic based on the contributions of Maritain and Niebuhr.

Outlines of the Just Society

What is the general outline of this social and political ethic that can serve the contemporary and ecumenical needs of humanity?

It must be an ethic relevant to both the social and individual character of humanity. The ideal of a just society can be summarized with the phrase "democratic pluralism and human rights." A *pluralist* society implies a differentiation of social forces and institutions—a diffusion of power through democratic means, utilizing checks and balances, but also a cooperation of these social forces for the sake of common interests. A society that respects *human rights* is one in which the balance of power between social groups operates to the benefit of each and every individual. In other words, the true service of the common good means realizing the true good of the individual: the rights to life and liberty, the right to political participation, the rights of the working person, including the right to enjoy the fruits of one's labors. Without the realization of these goals for the individual, no social system, not even one with a balance of forces, can claim to serve the common good. Furthermore, the rights of the individual necessarily imply a set of correlative responsibilities. In a just society, individuals must exercise and defend their rights. They must actively protect those rights and extend them to others. They must share a common, practical civic faith. As Maritain claims, they must have a mutual respect for truth, human dignity, freedom, and brotherly love—even while they differ on the theoretical foundations of these principles.[22]

This brief summary of the political ideal of "democratic pluralism and human rights" is one that is equally in tune with the work of both Maritain and Niebuhr. While it is perhaps true that Maritain gave more systematic and explicit expression to these principles, they are similarly the essential core of Niebuhr's political philosophy.

Reinhold Niebuhr is probably best remembered for his realistic assessment of the obstacles to a just society created by the "collective self-regard of class, race, and nation." He found this collective egoism "more stubborn and persistent than the egoism of individuals."[23] This was the thesis of his first major political

---

[22]Maritain, *Man and the State*, 111.

[23]Niebuhr, *Man's Nature and His Communities*, 22.

work, *Moral Man and Immoral Society*,[24] and it remained a persistent refrain. Over the course of many years and many books, Niebuhr developed a concept of society based on a realistic acceptance of power relationships and the necessity for restraining collective self-interest. He writes eloquently in defense of a society where power is placed in check by a pluralism of social forces utilizing the mechanisms of democracy. For Niebuhr, actual political power is always compounded with the ability to manipulate other forms of social power such as "military prowess, priestly prestige, economic ownership or . . . [control of] the technical processes of the community."[25] Most early empires were built on the concurrence or collaboration of priestly and military classes. The supreme achievement of modern civilizations, according to Niebuhr, is found in the differentiation of power.

> Modern democracies tend toward a more equal justice partly because they have divorced political power from special social functions. They endowed all men with a measure of it by giving them the right to review the policies of their leaders. This democratic principle does not obviate the formation of oligarchies in society; but it places a check upon their formation and upon the exercise of their power.[26]

Complementing Niebuhr's defense of democratic pluralism are the necessary corollaries of human rights, freedom, and responsibility. Niebuhr understood man's egoistic stubbornness, both individually and collectively, but he also appreciated man's essential dignity and his calling to greater realizations of his freedom. He saw in the respect for man's freedom and rights a fundamental good both for the individual and for society.

---

[24]Reinhold Niebuhr, *Moral Man and Immoral Society* (New York: Charles Scribner's Sons, Scribner Library, 1932).

[25]Reinhold Niebuhr, *Reflections on the End of an Era* (New York: Charles Scribner's Sons, 1934) 151.

[26]Reinhold Niebuhr, *The Nature and Destiny of Man: A Christian Interpretation*, 2 vols. (New York: Charles Scribner's Sons, Scribner Library, 1941-1943) 2:263.

Man requires freedom in his social organization because he is "essentially" free, which is to say that he has the capacity for indeterminate transcendence over the processes and limitations of nature. . . .

Both the individual and the community require freedom so that neither communal nor historical restraints may prematurely arrest the potencies which inhere in man's essential freedom and which express themselves collectively as well as individually.[27]

The freedom of man inherent in individual human beings was the logical foundation of equal political power—a power that was actualized through the right of suffrage, which was eventually extended to all adult citizens. That freedom was also the basis for equalizing opportunities and privileges in the economic sphere. Thus, over the course of time, democratic pluralist society was vindicated. Pluralism did not lead to chaos, as some political theorists had predicted, but to a balance of social forces and a respect for human rights, thus creating the conditions, at least potentially, for a just society. For Niebuhr, history revealed that "political encounters and debates in a free society involved not only contests of interests and power, but the rational engagement and enlargement of a native sympathy, a sense of justice, a residual moral integrity, and a sense of the common good in all classes of society."[28]

This is the general outline of Niebuhr's political ethic. It manifests a realistic approach to human nature and to the possibilities for realizing proximate justice in social relations. It includes a theory of political society that can be appropriately described as "democratic pluralist" and a theory of the individual citizen as endowed with human rights and civic responsibilities.

It is possible to summarize the political ethic of Jacques Maritain using a similar approach. He, too, preached an ideal of democratic pluralism and human rights. Maritain made what is probably his most significant contribution to political philosophy by his clear distinction between the state and the body politic

---

[27]Niebuhr, *The Children of Light and the Children of Darkness*, 3-4.

[28]Niebuhr, *Man's Nature and His Communities*, 68.

(or political society). Maritain attempted to show that the realm of politics encompasses every human concern of a temporal nature, and that the overt structures of government and political organizations are merely part of political society in general. That is to say, the state and the body politic are both concerned with the ethical, cultural, and rational endeavors of collective man; any difference between them lies in their scope.

> The state and the body politic . . . do not belong to two diverse categories, but they differ from each other as a part differs from the whole. The *Body Politic* or the *Political Society* is the whole. The state is a part—the topmost part—of this whole.[29]

The state is an institution with certain specific concerns—the maintenance of law, the promotion of common welfare, the administration of public affairs—through which it serves the larger whole of political society. The state, then, is a servant or instrument of the common good. Maritain contrasts this instrumentalist theory of the state with the absolutist or despotic theory in which the state is "super-imposed on the body politic or made to absorb the body politic altogether."[30]

Political society is a much more inclusive reality. It is made up of all of the institutions and common interests of the collectivity. It encompasses every political community within a nation.

> The body politic also contains in its superior unity the family units, whose essential rights and freedoms are anterior to itself, and a multiplicity of other particular societies which proceed from the free initiative of citizens. . . . Such is the element of pluralism inherent in every truly political society. Family, economic, cultural, educational, religious life matter as much as does political life to the very existence and prosperity of the body politic.[31]

So the body politic includes not only the state but every mediating institution that stands between it and the individual. And it

---

[29]Maritain, *Man and the State*, 9-10.

[30]Ibid., 14.

[31]Ibid., 11.

includes the free individual as well. Political society, for Maritain, requires a differentiation of social groupings in which each pursues its own proper ends. The ideal society is pluralistic, and it is animated by justice and brotherly love. As Maritain puts it, "Justice is a primary condition for the existence of the body politic, but Friendship is its very life-giving form."[32] Pluralism is the structure upon which a truly just society is built.

This theory of the body politic, and of the state as its instrument, is not unique to Maritain. It is one of the great treasures of Christian and humanist philosophy. It establishes the most radical and truly revolutionary idea in the whole realm of political life, the *limits* of the state. It is this idea that has so often stood between the rights of the common man and the will-to-power of the elites of various regimes throughout history. The idea of limited government provides a self-critical perspective that is sorely needed in the political life of a people.

Furthermore, the limited state and the pluralist body politic are the products of a particular development of modern social life, the democratic experiment. Maritain was one of the first Roman Catholic philosophers to discern the depth of compatibility of democracy with Christianity. He argues that modern industrialized society requires an organization in which civil authority arises from the will of the people. The broad masses must take on the responsibilities of self-government. This, according to Maritain, is because the Christian gospel affirms the fundamental freedom of every human person and calls them to greater realizations of that freedom. Maritain believed that democracy is the appropriate vehicle for a modern, just society inspired by Christian values. This is not to say that Christianity is tied to any particular type of social organization or historical era. It is not. The gospel is for all ages and all men. Christianity is not "linked to democracy"; rather, "democracy is linked to Christianity." The linkage operates in one principal direction. "The democratic impulse has arisen in human history as a temporal manifestation of the inspiration of the

---

[32]Ibid., 10.

Gospel."[33] In short, like Niebuhr, Maritain's notion of an ideal political society for the contemporary age can be summarized with the phrase "democratic pluralism." As for Niebuhr, so also for Maritain: human rights are inextricably tied to democratic pluralism.

The notion of pluralism implies the idea of a limited and instrumentalist state. It follows directly from this that every citizen is endowed with a set of inalienable rights: the rights of humanity as such, the political rights of the citizen, and the economic rights of the working person. The full realization of these rights is more likely in a pluralistic society, and less likely in an absolutist one, where a unitary configuration of power is established. But, for Maritain, human rights are rooted in something deeper still than the practical desirability of pluralism. He always expresses his definition of human rights in terms of the theory of natural law. "The philosophical foundation of human rights," he writes, "is Natural Law."[34]

The natural law is not a reified and static code, as it were, outside of man. It is an inner, dynamic, and progressive instrument for linking intellect and reality. The reality of man means that he is ordered toward certain ends—toward health, for example, and toward spirituality. The reality of life in man, the instinctual drive to preserve life, establishes by implication the right to life. The drive toward freedom in human beings establishes the right of freedom of action, within the bounds of respect for the rights of others. Likewise, the drive toward spiritual wholeness implies the right to the enjoyment of freedom of religion and conscience. Every state, therefore, must be judged according to whether it serves the common good by preserving the rights of its members, for these rights emerge from the very nature of man. Every modern political society that claims to be just must be comprised of a pluralism of social forces and institutions, democratically represented, with guarantees for the human rights of all its members.

---

[33]Jacques Maritain, *Christianity and Democracy*, trans. Doris C. Anson (New York: Charles Scribner's Sons, 1944) 37.

[34]Maritain, *Man and the State*, 80.

This, in brief, is the political ideal elaborated in the works of Jacques Maritain. It clearly shares a close affinity with the political ideal of Reinhold Niebuhr. There are differences between the two visions on particular issues, but these differences coincide with a general agreement or complementarity. Maritain and Niebuhr were tutored by the same set of historical experiences. Their ideals approximate what is best in the development of contemporary Western democracies. Still, each has a distinctive style as he expresses his political theology. Each understands the relationship of the spiritual and the temporal, the relationship of the two realms, in his own distinctive way.

Distinctive Styles of Political Theology

The question of the relationship between politics and religion, the problem of the two realms, is one that has a variety of solutions in Christian history. Maritain and Niebuhr elaborated the political ideal of freedom, but each did so in his own distinctive manner. The styles and rhythms of thought reflected in their work typify the classic Roman Catholic and Protestant approaches to the problem. In a broad sense, Maritain tended to emphasize the continuity rather than the discontinuity between God's law and man's, between the sacred and the secular. Niebuhr generally tended to emphasize the discontinuity, or the ways in which human society contradicted the law of love.

The idea of the continuity or discontinuity of the two realms was subjected to rigorous scholarly analysis by H. Richard Niebuhr, the brother of Reinhold Niebuhr, in a book entitled *Christ and Culture*.[35] While I will not attempt to describe the typology that H. Richard Niebuhr constructed, I have adapted his ideas in order to name the styles represented by Maritain and Niebuhr, respectively. Maritain represents the "analogic" relation between the two realms, while Niebuhr exemplifies the "paradoxic" relation.

---

[35]H. Richard Niebuhr, *Christ and Culture* (New York: Harper & Bros., Harper Torchbooks, 1956).

An approach that emphasizes the continuity of the sacred and the secular posits a possible synthesis of the two, an analogous relation. Maritain's conceptual model involves a hierarchy in which the higher, supernatural realm of religion completes and perfects the lower, natural realm of culture. The two realms are ultimately compatible, although their differences are acknowledged.

Niebuhr's approach emphasizes the discontinuities between sacred norms and worldly realities, and its posits a perpetual tension between the two, a paradoxic relation. Niebuhr's conceptual model involves an affirmation of a substantial tension between religion and culture, of their relative autonomy, and of the dual obligation of every individual—the obligation to God and the obligation to society. The two realms exist in enduring tension, although they are not totally opposed.

These concepts provide a method for contrasting the particular styles of thought that distinguished Jacques Maritain and Reinhold Niebuhr while, at the same time, pointing to their underlying similarities. Both analogy and paradox are valid approaches to the interpretation of Jesus' commandment regarding the things that are Caesar's and the things that are God's. The relationship between God and man, sacred and secular, eternal and temporal, religion and politics, is a complex one. As H. Richard Niebuhr shows, other Christian approaches exist besides those represented by Jacques Maritain and Reinhold Niebuhr. Each contributes something to our understanding of the mystery of the two realms. Ultimately, it is necessary for Christian political theology in an ecumenical age to recognize and to assimilate the truth of each strand of its tradition.

Maritain and Niebuhr both made lifelong attempts to delineate a doctrine of the two realms—a political theology, as I have defined this term. In the process of seeking to connect the divine order with the earthly, political order, they came to profess a belief in democratic pluralism and human rights and to elaborate a theology of freedom. It would be enough to understand in a new way the special contributions to the Christian tradition that these two twentieth-century theologians have left us. But there is even greater benefit if, by taking them both together, we discover the outlines of an ecumenical political theology that encompasses the collective wisdom of Christian civilization.

Practical Wisdom
and Realism
in Politics

> Common inherited experience and the moral and intellectual instincts . . . constitute a kind of empirical, practical wisdom, much deeper and denser and much nearer the hidden complex dynamism of human life than any artificial construction of reason.

> Jacques Maritain
> Man and the State[1]

---

[1](Chicago: University of Chicago Press, 1951) 11.

II

Maritain and Niebuhr were intellectual shapers of the contemporary mind; their contributions to philosophy and theology were extremely diverse, from aesthetics to psychology, epistemology, and logic. In addition, both devoted substantial energies to sociocultural studies and political ethics. Both are remembered for their many political writings in defense of freedom, equality, and responsible self-government. In their own distinctive ways, both made the concepts of human rights and democratic pluralism understandable in our modern world.

In the dismal 1930s, Maritain dreamt of a "new world" and a new kind of freedom.

> In order that there should succeed to capitalist civilization in decadence a new world superior to Communism, nothing less is required than the personalist and integral humanist principle in its widest significance, nothing less than the energies of spiritual and social resurrection of which man does not become capable by the grace of the State, but by a love which vivifies his freedom as a

person, and which fixes the center of his life infinitely above the State.[2]

This personalist view of man in relation to the state was at the heart of Maritain's practical wisdom. Similarly, Niebuhr spoke with a voice of realism in a politically chaotic world.

> All power is a peril to justice. . . . Democracy, whatever its limitations, is a necessary check upon the imperialism of oligarchs, whether communistic or capitalistic.[3]

Both of these short statements appeared in print during a troubled time, 1935-1936, in which extremisms of the left and the right imperiled justice and freedom. Both contain within them the seeds of a more fully fleshed political ethic relevant to the world that emerged from this tragic period. In Maritain's ideas of "personalism" and "practical wisdom" and Niebuhr's concepts of "realism" and "justice," there lies a rationale for a contemporary politics, a politics of deep compassion and of responsible power.

In comparing Maritain and Niebuhr, and their political philosophies, one is confronted with a curious affinity. Politically, the two theologians seem surprisingly compatible; they appear to have shared a common ground on many issues of public policy facing the Western democracies. They showed a parallel interest in the themes of human rights, the common good, positive social change, and civic faith. Yet, as theologians and as political participants, they emerged from distinct milieux and served as spokesmen for different traditions. In many ways Maritain and Niebuhr were, respectively, typically Roman Catholic and Protestant. Their personal differences embodied this classic division within Christianity. How, then, can the apparent affinity in practical political matters be explained?

---

[2]Jacques Maritain, *Integral Humanism: Temporal and Spiritual Problems of a New Christendom*, trans. Joseph W. Evans (New York: Charles Scribner's Sons, 1968; rpt., Notre Dame IN: University of Notre Dame Press, 1973) 279.

[3]Reinhold Niebuhr, *An Interpretation of Christian Ethics* (New York: Harper & Bros., 1935; rpt., New York: Meridian Books, Living Age Books, 1956) 171.

If it is true that Maritain and Niebuhr had similar views on social and political matters, while representing distinctly different political instincts or styles, then it may be possible to understand their affinity as an affinity of opposites, a complementarity. Although the Roman Catholic and Protestant types of Christian political theory are stylistically distinct—perhaps as much for cultural reasons as for theological reasons—they both reflect a common set of principles, leading to a common political program. This generically "Christian" bedrock of principles is centered upon the virtues of prudence, justice, and love; the doctrines of divine judgment and human responsibility; and the doctrine of a natural law binding the reality of the temporal world with the deeper reality of the spiritual realm. These Christian principles lie at the center of the political philosophies of both Maritain and Niebuhr. This common set of principles could be called "biblical myth," or more precisely, "biblical eschatology," since it represents the theological expression of meaning in history. The virtues, and the doctrines of divine judgment and natural law, help to make history—especially political history, both past and present—meaningful for Christians. Such theological expressions of meaning in history, or any similar expressions, provide politics with its ground of self-understanding and make possible a responsible social activism. Thus Maritain and Niebuhr developed their understanding of politics in relation to a theological view of the world—specifically, a theological view of nature and history.

The common Christian presuppositions that inform the political philosophies of Maritain and Niebuhr are expressed in their writings in typically Roman Catholic and Protestant ways. Maritain sought to adapt Thomist philosophy, including political philosophy, to the modern era, to update it for a new situation. In that sense, he is rightly called a "neo-Thomist." Part of his intention for a renewed Roman Catholic political philosophy can be seen in the title of one of his books, *The Rights of Man and Natural Law*. In other words, he sought to show how a contemporary human rights philosophy could be grounded in traditional Roman Catholic social teaching, rightly understood. Niebuhr similarly reflected his background as a Protestant, emphasizing the importance of the self-critical method and the doctrine of original sin as they apply to contemporary social ethics. He criticized both the orthodox and liberal schools in a bid to restate authentic Christian social teaching. In that sense, he is correctly called a "neo-orthodox" theologian. Ultimately, though, their stylistic or methodological differences, along with their convergence on matters of policy, account for the complementarity of their political philosophies.

Key Interpretative Concepts

The central core of the political philosophies and social ethics of Maritain and Niebuhr is to be found in the key interpretative concepts that inform their work, and that are closely related to the key ethical virtues emphasized in their systems. For Maritain the fundamental concept is "practical wisdom"; the key virtue, "prudence." For Niebuhr the fundamental concept is "realism," corresponding to the key virtues of "justice and love" in creative tension. These terms represent the distinctive characteristics of their respective social-ethical systems, providing the depth dimension to each position they took on particular practical issues. In the final analysis, these *theoretical* foundations provide the basis for establishing and legitimating the *practical* policies of respect for human rights and democratic pluralism. Taken as a whole, this set of concepts provides the outline of an ecumenical social ethic for modern, free society.

These two fundamental concepts of Maritain and Niebuhr, in fact, denote interpretative skills. An interpretative skill is a technique for *knowing* and *deciding;* it is a capacity for sound judgment. In the political sphere such skills are the mark of great leaders, politicians, and statesmen. Political leadership requires understanding and shrewdness, the fabled Solomonic wisdom. Politics also demands realism, such as that embodied in the checks and balances of Jeffersonian democracy. Politics is both the art of the possible and the drive toward perfect justice. Thus it is the arena of successful and failed attempts to establish proximate justice within given, contingent situations. Naturally, success builds a politician's reputation for sound judgment. But, successful or not, we recognize and honor true insight and discernment in leaders who correctly perceive and courageously defend the common good. Political discernment is difficult to define, but it is indispensable to human survival and peaceful coexistence.

Virtue is closely related to sound judgment. Virtue gives sound judgment its direction and ultimate purpose, its *telos*, by making values the criteria of sound judgment. The primary social values include life, human dignity, freedom, and community. Therefore, truly great political leaders are seen as embodiments of public virtue and as defenders of the values of the community. Not only leaders, but ordinary citizens as well, may exhibit this characteristic of sound judgment capped by virtue. Modern, open societies—the practical approximation of the ideal of democratic pluralism—depend upon the sound judgment and virtue of their leadership *and* citizenry for their very survival. Unquestionably, interpretative skills and humane values must be given central importance in analyzing political philosophies.

The fundamental concepts and epistemological presuppositions of theologians have typically been classified according to the relative importance each places on "reason" and "revelation." Yet this can be only an initial step toward uncovering the underlying structure of thought reflected by such ideas as "natural law" or "the tragic dimension of history." Maritain and Niebuhr were both committed Christians and professional theologians. As such, the biblical narrative infused their writings with a distinct prophetic quality. "Reason" and "revelation" were combined in complex and unique ways in their respective world views; the distinctiveness of each man's conceptual style emerges from the depths of meaning contained in each one's fundamental concept.

It is probably impossible to give a single definition that would do full justice to the meaning of *both* practical wisdom and realism. One might begin to approach this problem by asking, "What is the nature of political leadership and responsibility?" To give a negative definition, one that is roughly appropriate to both central concepts, we might answer by saying that we are concerned with the key political virtue or capacity without which a people inevitably falls prey to the illusions of power, to the distortions of their own injustices, and to the cunning and tragic twists of history. Niebuhr is perhaps best remembered for his ability to expose such illusions, injustices, ironies, and tragedies in the political histories of nations—his own as well as others. Maritain's own awareness of such intractable political realities is perhaps best shown in his *The Peasant of the Garonne*,[4] where we see his realism, and even pessimism, about the lack of progress made during his lifetime toward the ideal of a "New Christendom" of political justice.

Both men saw and exposed with particular clarity the political illusions and injustices of their times. By exercising a political sensibility that was prudent and realistic, each offered concrete, historical explanations and solutions for the problems of the era. They both lived in a century of great upheaval, wars, genocide, and totalitarian expansionism. Their reasoned and persistent defense of freedom may have helped to prevent even greater disasters.

One might say that "practical wisdom" or "realism" is the capacity to *understand* power, to form political *judgments*, and to *act* on the basis of a moral critique of power. These key terms suggest an appreciation for man's rational and moral possibilities tempered by a realism about man's sinfulness and will-to-power. This world view is characterized by a major emphasis on self-criticism and self-restraint. It is based upon a realistic view of individuals and of collective humanity. Maritain and Niebuhr acknowledge the necessity of established political authority, and they acknowledge its rational and moral potentialities. Yet they unflaggingly call for the critique of all power from a transcendent perspective. In this the two theologians reflect the traditional and predominant Christian attitude toward politics and the state: qualified loyalty to a legitimate and sufficiently just government, but ultimate loyalty to God alone. This is the bedrock of Christian political theory in both Roman Catholicism and Protestantism.

In the Christian view "the world" is an ambiguous realm, neither wholly good nor wholly evil. Christians are to be responsible and worldly while at the same time critical and otherworldly. Thus

---

[4]Jacques Maritain, *The Peasant of the Garonne: An Old Layman Questions Himself about the Present Time*, trans. Michael Cuddihy and Elizabeth Hughes (New York: Holt, Rinehart & Winston, 1968; rpt., New York: Macmillan Co., 1969) see esp. chs. 1 and 2.

Christianity preaches a moral critique of power, a qualified loyalty to the state, and a creative tension with the world. Niebuhr expresses this view succinctly.

> There is no "Christian" economic or political system. But there is a Christian attitude toward all systems and schemes of justice. It consists on the one hand of a *critical attitude* toward the claims of all systems and schemes, expressed in the question whether they will contribute to justice in a concrete situation; and on the other hand a *responsible attitude,* which will not pretend to be God nor refuse to make a decision between political answers to a problem because each answer is discovered to contain a moral ambiguity in God's sight. We are men, not God; we are responsible for making choices between greater and lesser evils, even when our Christian faith, illuminating the human scene, makes it quite apparent that there is no pure good in history; and probably no pure evil either. The fate of civilizations may depend upon these choices between systems of which some are more, others less, just.[5]

Maritain often made statements similar to Niebuhr's concerning the ambiguities of practical politics. In a passage in *The Peasant of the Garonne,* he conveys the moral critique of power in much more symbolic and cosmic terms than Niebuhr customarily used.

> The world is the domain *at once* of man, of God, and of the devil. Thus appears the essential ambiguity of the world and of its history; it is a field common to the three. The world is a closed field which belongs to God by right of creation; to the devil by right of conquest, because of sin; to Christ by right of victory over the conqueror, because of the Passion. The task of the Christian in the world is to contend with the devil his domain, to wrest it from him; he must strive to this end, he will succeed in it only in part as long as time will endure. The world is saved, yes, it is delivered in *hope,* it is on the march toward the kingdom of God definitely revealed; but it is not *holy,* it is the Church which is holy; it is on the march toward the kingdom of God, and this is why it

---

[5]Reinhold Niebuhr, *Faith and Politics: A Commentary on Religious, Social and Political Thought in a Technological Age,* ed. Ronald H. Stone (New York: George Braziller, 1968) 56 (emphasis added).

is a treason toward his kingdom not to seek with all one's forces—in a manner adapted to the conditions of earthly history, but as effective as possible, *quantum potes, tantum aude*—a realization, or, more exactly, a refraction in the world of the Gospel exigencies; nevertheless, this realization, even though relative, will always be in one manner or another deficient and disputed in the world. And at the same time that the history of the world is on the march—it is the growth of the wheat—toward the kingdom of God, it is also on the march—it is the growth of the tares, inextricably mingled with the wheat—toward the kingdom of reprobation.[6]

These two statements—one by Niebuhr, the other by Maritain—epitomize the fundamentally Christian attitude toward the world, which is one of creative tension. At bottom the two views are similar, but in their elaboration of these ideals, Maritain and Niebuhr shape this tension between God and the world in distinctively Roman Catholic and Protestant ways.

"Practical wisdom" and "realism," even though not identical, are closely related concepts. Both concern truthful judgment, especially in political affairs. From different perspectives, each concept can be said to include and transcend the other. Maritain and Niebuhr employ these concepts in a number of distinct ways; and, even when their words are identical, one cannot be sure that their meaning is too. Great care is called for in comparing the two. Both philosophers take pains to establish the significance of the highest and most inclusive interpretative technique or political virtue, and to make it the essence of their respective systems. So, to compare Maritain and Niebuhr is to compare the concepts of practical wisdom and realism, and the role they play in the discernment of political realities.

Maritain's Concept of Practical Wisdom

Practical wisdom, for Maritain, is the fundamental concept and the key interpretative skill in matters of a practical, worldly nature. Practical wisdom is correlative to "prudence," the political virtue par excellence. Insight and a virtuous will are but two as-

---

[6]Maritain, *The Peasant of the Garonne*, 47-48.

pects of a single human characteristic. They should, but do not always, go together. Practical wisdom can be defined as the knowledge of the judgments and actions that are most appropriate to a given, concrete situation in human society. Since it implies the virtue of prudence, practical wisdom is also the will to carry out these "most appropriate" judgments and actions.

Maritain frequently reminds us that "practical reason . . . is the measure of human acts."[7] He always took great care to distinguish the human and practical from the divine and theoretical, devoting voluminous writings to "theoretical wisdom" as well as to ethics and politics. The difference between practical and theoretical wisdom, as well as the fundamental qualities that comprise a mature capacity for practical wisdom, are evident in his oft-quoted thesis regarding international cooperation.

> Men possessing quite different, even opposite, metaphysical or religious outlooks, can converge, not by virtue of any identity of doctrine, but by virtue of an ideological similitude in practical principles, toward the same practical conclusions, and can share in the same practical secular faith, provided that they revere, perhaps for quite diverse reasons, truth and intelligence, human dignity, freedom, brotherly love, and the absolute value of moral good.[8]

Practical wisdom is moral intelligence, true insight with true conscience; it is prudent judgment.

The concept of practical wisdom is basic to Thomistic philosophy. Thomism encompasses a political philosophy based on man's rational capacities; it is a view of the world as a flawed reflection of the divine order. Hence man, through his rational capabilities, should (but may not) devise social structures which embody the natural law that is manifest in man, especially in his conscience. Although these social structures are rational—that is, consonant with God's mind and the best human reasoning—they are, nevertheless, instruments of partial justice in a fallen world.

---

[7]Maritain, *Man and the State*, 89.

[8]Ibid., 111.

Thomistic political theory was originally associated with the temporarily unified civilization of medieval European Christendom, but it is a theory adaptable to other situations, including that of pluralistic societies. Maritain recovered Thomistic rationalism and realism, and explained its relevance for the modern, pluralistic world. His political theory reflects the philosophical method perfected by Thomas Aquinas—not in the dry, positivistic manner of some Thomist thinkers, but in the dynamic and personalist manner of Aquinas himself. One can sense in Maritain's writings his pain over the state of Thomism and his intense desire to rescue Aquinas for a world greatly in need of his broad vision. By rescuing Thomism from its literalizers and drawing out its modern implications, Maritain became the leading neo-Thomist political philosopher of the twentieth century.

The idea of practical wisdom entered the Thomistic system through Thomas's rediscovery of Aristotle. Aristotle was the originator of the concept of *phronesis*,[9] the skill or capacity of "well-acting." This Greek term denotes a certain skill, or grace, which characterizes artistic excellence as well as moral excellence. It is the skill or capacity of true judgment and proper timing. The terms *prudence* and *providence* derive from the Latin *phronesis*. Aristotle thought of *phronesis* as an active verb, like the archer's skill of "hitting the mark." He held that *phronesis* was the precondition of virtuous action, or action-for-good—"virtue" and "the good" being derived from a single root, *aretē*. Whereas most people choose from a spectrum of options between two moral extremes, Aristotle looked for the "mean above the extremes." This was not the mean between extremes, but the mean above the spectrum, which combines the best of both extremes and of the intermediate positions as well. *Phronesis* is the skill to discover this mean and act upon it. The Golden Mean is a rich and subtle concept, one of the earliest and best examples of the use of the dialectical principle in philosophy.

---

[9]Aristotle, *Nicomachean Ethics*, trans. Martin Ostwald (Indianapolis: Bobbs-Merrill, Library of Liberal Arts, 1962) see esp. 152-54.

The *phronimos*, the man or woman who possesses this skill of judgment, is one whose decisions and actions prove to be wise and virtuous in actual practice. Aristotle cited the example of Pericles, the great fifth-century Athenian statesman, as one who possessed this skill of judgment.[10] Other examples of men of practical wisdom include King Solomon of ancient Israel, King Louis IX of France—a contemporary of Thomas, whom G. K. Chesterton described as "one of those men in whom a certain simplicity, combined with courage and activity, makes it natural, and in a sense easy, to fulfill directly and promptly any duty or office"[11]—and Winston Churchill, who was considered by Reinhold Niebuhr to be the preeminent realist of the twentieth century.[12] *Phronesis*, then, is an embodied characteristic or potentiality of human nature. It is a real quality that manifests itself in given, existential situations. Practical wisdom and realism encompass both theory and practice.

Charity and Prudence: Maritain on the Virtues

The Thomistic philosophy worked out in the *Summa Theologica* makes extensive use of Artistotle's concept of *phronesis*. Thomas took the Greek idea of well-acting and the notion of Christian virtue and combined them in the term *charity*, which he then made the fundamental ideal of his moral philosophy. Charity is at least as important a concept as natural law in the Thomistic ethic. Charity is, for Thomas, a habit created in the human soul and infused therein by grace such that the soul voluntarily seeks the good, including the highest good, which is God. As such, charity is the most powerful of the virtues and is, in fact, the very form of all other virtues. Since the object of charity is the

---

[10]Ibid., 153.

[11]G. K. Chesterton, *Saint Thomas Aquinas* (London: Sheed & Ward, 1933; rpt., Garden City NY: Doubleday & Co., Image Books, 1956) 98.

[12]See Reinhold Niebuhr, *The Self and the Dramas of History* (New York: Charles Scribner's Sons, 1955) 214.

highest good, charity is not an ordinary virtue but is itself the highest virtue.[13]

Thomistic moral philosophy, based on the habit and virtue of charity, is the basis for Maritain's understanding of politics and social relations. Maritain takes up the tradition of *phronesis* and charity by constructing a moral philosophy that has as its basis the concepts of practical wisdom and prudence, which, in turn, belong to broader, traditional Christian teaching concerning the virtues.

The doctrine of the virtues begins with the distinction between two types of virtues: theological virtues and cardinal virtues. The theological virtues—faith, hope, and love—have God for their direct object. They signify faith in divine revelation, hope for divine salvation, and love for the divine Father. Each virtue is a gift of God, not a solely human achievement. The cardinal virtues, by contrast, find their direct object in human action, in moral striving. They are prudence, justice, courage, and temperance.[14] Each of the cardinal virtues is, likewise, a result of divine grace and not merely a product of human effort. The highest of the cardinal virtues, and the one that incorporates each of the others, is prudence. Thus prudence signifies the perfection of justice, temperance, and fortitude, just as love contains the other two theological virtues of faith and hope.

The exercise of prudence means that an act is willed with due consideration to *justice* in all its dimensions. A prudent ruler will act in a way that is informed by concern for the rights and responsibilities of all parties. Prudence implies fortitude or *courage* as well as justice. Political fortitude is the virtue of defending what is right and true. It is courage in public matters. But not every act of courage is virtuous; only courage in defense of truth counts as such. Maritain notes,

---

[13]Thomas Aquinas, *On Charity*, trans. Lottie H. Kendzierski, Medieval Philosophical Texts in Translation, no. 10 (Milwaukee: Marquette University Press, 1960) 33-39.

[14]See Josef Pieper, *The Four Cardinal Virtues: Prudence, Justice, Fortitude, Temperance* (Notre Dame IN: University of Notre Dame Press, 1966).

Fortitude is a cardinal virtue in so far as it inclines and steadies the will of man to meet and overcome difficulties that are in conflict with the claims of justice and with the life of reason and truth. . . . [It is] directed to the firm and loyal defense of right against every kind of evil.[15]

He goes on to point out that the main ingredient in fortitude is not aggression, but endurance, suffering with constancy, the courage to defend truth through self-sacrifice.[16] The prudent ruler acts with courage in the preservation of justice. Finally, prudence implies *temperance*, that balance of judgment which takes account of all factors. The temperate ruler renders an even-handed and level-headed decision based on the facts and a rational appraisal of the complete situation.

Prudence is the quality of decision and act in which justice, fortitude, temperance, and practical wisdom are each given their proper place. The relation of practical wisdom to prudence and the other cardinal virtues is the key to understanding Maritain's ethics. Maritain depicts this relation in broad strokes in his discussion of freedom and the acting person. "According to St. Thomas," Maritain writes, "speculative science has knowledge itself for its intrinsic end. . . . Practical science has for its intrinsic end something other than mere knowledge: its knowledge is for action." This is the first basic division in science or philosophy. Ethics belongs to the practical order, the order which demands that knowledge be put to the test of action. Just as first principles play a primary role in speculative science, the ends of human life—the first principles of morality—are the primary concern of ethics. The science of ethics "examines and utilizes a great mass of material alike of the speculative and of the experimental order." It then

---

[15]Jacques Maritain, *Freedom in the Modern World*, trans. Richard O'Sullivan (New York: Charles Scribner's Sons, 1936; rpt., New York: Gordian Press, 1971) 172.

[16]Maritain's admiring account of the *Satyagraha* techniques of M. K. Gandhi, as well as his objections to the "idealism and unrealism that are inherent in [Gandhi's] doctrine," are recorded ibid., 168-72, and appendix 2.

"seeks to know what is right to be done, and how it may be done so that it shall be done well."[17]

Ethics is the science of freedom, a practical science exploring the use of free will. However, because ethics is a philosophy of human action, a science, it is not finally a guarantee of correct judgment; something more is needed.

> I need a means of knowledge and of practical judgment that is more than a science. I need the virtue of prudence: a virtue that resides in the reason but is also of the moral order, seeing that it can only judge rightly if the will too is rectified; for prudence controls the exercise of my freedom immediately, not from a distance. Prudence is integrated with the other moral virtues; it presupposes that I know what justice and what temperance require not merely by way of theory but in an experimental way by the connatural knowledge that comes of the habitual exercise of these virtues.[18]

Prudence is that combination of virtues which leads to right conduct, that combination of "stable dispositions which will prepare and fortify us to make a right use of our freedom."[19]

Maritain's Dynamic View of Natural Law

With a firm understanding of the central role of practical wisdom and prudence in Maritain's systematic political theology, it is possible to turn to his explanation of the complex interaction of intellect and will, which leads to moral action in social and political life. This aspect of the problem is the key to understanding the role of natural law in the guidance of human action. For Maritain, the will is "an original spiritual energy of infinite capacity which has control over the intelligence." Nevertheless, the will depends upon intellect for its specification; "the will can do nothing without a judgment by the intellect." Thus the free act is an event in which "the intelligence and will involve and enve-

---

[17]Ibid., 20-21.

[18]Ibid., 22.

[19]Ibid.

lope each other vitally."[20] This relationship is a key part of Maritain's explanation of the metaphysical mystery of human personality: will controls intellect, but intellect determines will.

This concept of will and intellect in tandem dictates, according to Maritain, a correct view of the doctrine of natural law. The natural law is not a fixed, pre-existent code of norms to which man, through his intellect, must conform. This law of nature is not outside of man but within his very soul. The natural law guides human action through the dynamic relationship of intellect and will, practical wisdom and prudence. A prudent judgment is an existential event, an act of freedom in which conscience and soul discover a *natural* pathway to justice—that is, one that conforms to human nature. Natural law, Maritain persistently argues, is the measure of practical reason, the measure of human acts. He defines natural law as "an order . . . which human reason can discover and according to which the human will must act in order to attune itself to the necessary ends of the human being."[21]

The basis of natural law is expressed in Aquinas's dictum to do good and avoid evil. Maritain writes, "The only practical knowledge all men have naturally and infallibly in common as a self-evident principle, intellectually perceived by virtue of the concepts involved, is that we must do good and avoid evil." Of course, this is only the first step. "This is the preamble and the principle of natural law; it is not the law itself."[22] The reasoning here goes back through Aquinas to Aristotle, Plato, and Socrates. That good is to be sought and evil avoided follows from their very definitions.

Second, "Natural law is an unwritten law. Man's knowledge of it has increased little by little as man's moral conscience has

---

[20]Jacques Maritain, *The Social and Political Philosophy of Jacques Maritain: Selected Readings*, trans. Joseph W. Evans and Leo R. Ward (New York: Charles Scribner's Sons, 1955; rpt., Notre Dame IN: University of Notre Dame Press, 1976) 13.

[21]Jacques Maritain, *The Rights of Man and Natural Law*, trans. Doris C. Anson (New York: Charles Scribner's Sons, 1943; rpt., New York: Gordian Press, 1971) 61

[22]Maritain, *Man and the State*, 90.

developed." Our current state of awareness is still imperfect, awaiting fuller penetration by the gospel spirit. The natural law is only known as it is brought to human consciousness and is promulgated. "It is only insofar as it is known and expressed in assertions of practical reason that natural law has force of law."[23]

Third, "Human reason does not discover the regulations of natural law in an abstract and theoretical manner, as a series of geometrical theorems."[24] The correct understanding of natural law is not positivistic but dynamic. Maritain's discussion is illuminating.

> I think that Thomas Aquinas' teaching, here, should be understood in a much deeper and more precise fashion than is usual. When he says that human reason discovers the regulations of natural law through the guidance of the *inclinations* of human nature, he means that the very mode or manner in which human reason knows natural law is not rational knowledge, but knowledge *through inclination.* That kind of knowledge is not clear knowledge through concepts and conceptual judgments; it is obscure, unsystematic, vital knowledge by connaturality or congeniality, in which the intellect, in order to bear judgment, consults and listens to the inner melody that the vibrating strings of abiding tendencies make present in the subject.[25]

After all, Maritain argues, the natural law has been discovered and

---

[23]Ibid., 90-91.

[24]Ibid., 91.

[25]Ibid., 91-92. Similarly, Joseph Fuchs argues that "St. Thomas Aquinas underlines the mutability of human nature and consequently admits a variability of the natural law (in a historical and material although not 'metaphysical' and formal way)." See his *Natural Law: A Theological Investigation*, trans. Helmut Reckter and John A. Dowling (New York: Sheed & Ward, 1965) 111; see also 92-95. Paul Ramsey suggests that "there is a close parallel between what Maritain means by knowledge through inclination . . . and Niebuhr's belief that because of freedom and man's self-understanding in the moment of transcendence 'all human life is informed with an inchoate sense of responsibility toward the ultimate law of life—the law of love.' " See his *Nine Modern Moralists* (Englewood Cliffs NJ: Prentice-Hall, 1962; rpt., New York: New American Library, Mentor Books, 1970) 158; quoting Niebuhr, *An Interpretation of Christian Ethics*, 112.

rediscovered in social communities from ancient times to the present; it is not merely a product of individual judgments.

Maritain's understanding of the dynamism of natural law explains why there is both a universal aspect in law and an immense variety of rules, customs, and standards.[26] Practical wisdom taps the resources of a natural law rooted in concrete historical experience. As the political skill of knowing the appropriate response to a given situation, practical wisdom is the result of a deep awareness of the community's vision of the natural law at a given point in its history. The leader who acts in accord with this commonly held natural law and deepens its meaning is the *phronimos*, the man of practical wisdom.

Proceeding to further clarify the concept of natural law, Maritain remarks that the development of the concept has proceeded from an emphasis on obligations to an emphasis on rights. Without worshiping progress, Maritain affirms the reality of progress, as well as decline, in human history. "Progress of moral conscience is indeed the most unquestionable instance of progress in humanity."[27] Different ages are responsible for different contributions.

> In ancient and medieval times attention was paid, in natural law, to the *obligations* of man more than to his *rights*. The proper achievement indeed—of the XVIIIth century has been to bring out in full light the *rights* of man as also required by natural law.[28]

Unfortunately, however, the new awareness of rights as part of the natural law of human social existence led, in many cases, to the exclusion of considerations of obligations. Freedom led to permissiveness. Maritain was a staunch defender of a concept of natural law that encompasses both rights and obligations. The skill of practical wisdom must have its foundation in this comprehensive view of the natural law.

---

[26]Ibid., 93.

[27]Ibid., 94.

[28]Ibid.

Finally, the concept of natural law, and the correlative qualities of practical wisdom and prudence, lead to a full-blown vision of human rights as fundamental to justice in the contemporary world. In a long passage in *The Rights of Man and Natural Law*, Maritain shows how the notion of human dignity is both logically and historically rooted in a personal and collective awareness of natural law.[29] Practical wisdom in politics perceives the connections between communal notions of natural law and the fundamental rights inherent in each member of the community. The true statesman exercises a precise judgment with regard to the defense of human rights in every particular situation. The list of enumerated rights and duties grows with the moral development of the community through time. So also do the mechanisms by which self-government and communal unity-in-diversity grow. The end result for the free societies of the contemporary Western world is a civilization whose gospel roots have produced democratic pluralism and a persistent defense of human rights. Thus the basic concept of practical wisdom is expressed in social and political practice.[30]

Maritain's approach to all philosophical matters in the practical order is to seek practical wisdom based on natural law, as it is existentially and realistically conceived. He frequently and explicitly discusses his methodology of practical wisdom, whatever the particular subject under discussion. In every case his approach is consistent with the Aristotelian tradition of *phronesis* and the Thomistic ideal of charity. "The metaphysics which I hold to be founded on truth may be described as a critical realism and as a philosophy of intelligence and of being, or still more precisely as a philosophy of the *act of existing* regarded as the act and perfection of all perfections, these formulas, of course, will be of interest only to specialists."[31] Practical wisdom is important for political philosophy because it is the skill of analyzing, judging, and acting according to an evolving but "natural" concept of jus-

---

[29]Maritain, *The Rights of Man and Natural Law*, 58-73.

[30]For further elaboration on this theme, see ch. 4.

[31]Maritain, *The Social and Political Philosophy of Jacques Maritain*, 334.

tice. Practical wisdom preserves and expands the dimensions of justice embodied in natural law. It is the intellectual counterpart of the virtue of prudence.

Together, the notions of practical wisdom, prudence, and natural law constitute a framework for the political philosophy of democratic pluralism and human rights, the theology of freedom. The similarities between Maritain's use of "practical wisdom" and Niebuhr's use of "realism" will become apparent in the discussion of Niebuhr's key interpretative technique. Although Niebuhr frequently criticized the static quality of arguments based on the natural law tradition, it should become obvious that his goal was the same as Maritain's: to set forth a dynamic view of the human struggle to understand and to establish the just society.

Niebuhr's Concept of Realism

The fundamental concept of political theology, the key interpretative technique for knowing and deciding in matters of a political nature, according to Niebuhr, is realism. He frequently contrasts realism with the extremes of idealism or sentimentality, on the one hand, and cynicism, on the other. He uses the phrase "Christian realism" to signify a political style that takes seriously the biblical view of man both as corrupted by sin and potentially reconciled to God, others, and self. In the 1930s and 1940s, the young Niebuhr's commitment to Marxism steadily eroded and was replaced by a biblical view of human nature and destiny. The biblical myth seemed to him to be a truer myth leading to a better praxis.[32] Niebuhr's realism is best expressed not merely by his criticism of moralistic attitudes and utopian schemes but also by his progressive social ethic based on the key virtues of justice and love in creative tension.

Niebuhr defined political realism as the capacity to take seriously those human characteristics that do not fit neatly into a ra-

[32]Dennis McCann, "Reinhold Niebuhr and Jacques Maritain on Marxism: A Comparison of Two Traditional Models of Practical Theology," *Journal of Religion* 58 (April 1978): 147. See also Roger C. Hutchinson, "Reinhold Niebuhr and 'Contextual Connections,' " and the response by John H. Berthong in *This World*, no. 6 (Fall 1983): 102-14.

tional and optimistic scheme of social organization. "In political moral theory 'realism' denotes the disposition to take all factors in a social and political situation, which offer resistance to established norms, into account, particularly the factors of self-interest and power."[33] Idealism, on the other hand, is considered both by its proponents and its critics to be a disposition of loyalty to moral norms and ideals. But, however much we might admire the idealist, his disposition, according to Niebuhr, underestimates the self-righteous and self-deceiving tendencies in all moral endeavor. The disposition to idealism "is general whenever men are inclined to take the moral pretensions of themselves or their fellow men at face value; for the disposition to hide self-interest behind the façade of pretended devotion to values, transcending self-interest, is well-nigh universal."[34] These definitions emphasize dispositions, Niebuhr points out, and are therefore to be used cautiously as inexact but useful concepts.

Realism is further distinguished from idealism in its attitude toward history. The realist believes that "certain perennial problems of political organization emerge in new forms" as tribe becomes city-state and city-state becomes nation. This is the basic theme of Niebuhr's *The Structure of Nations and Empires.* The struggle for political integration and long-term viability is the same struggle in various stages and eras of history; some form of imperialism, for example, is a permanent fixture of political life. The realist discovers perennial problems in new forms. The idealist is "conscious of novel and radical elements in a new situation," and he tends to believe or hope that old problems will vanish as new political strata are reached.[35] Clearly, Niebuhr sketches these distinctions with the intention of showing the superiority of realism to idealism.

---

[33]Reinhold Niebuhr, *Christian Realism and Political Problems* (New York: Charles Scribner's Sons, 1953; rpt., Fairfield NJ: Augustus M. Kelley, 1977) 119.

[34]Ibid., 120.

[35]Reinhold Niebuhr, *Reinhold Niebuhr on Politics: His Political Philosophy and Its Application to Our Age as Expressed in His Writings,* ed. Harry R. Davis and Robert C. Wood (New York: Charles Scribner's Sons, 1960) 65.

Ultimately, the difference between realists and idealists comes down to a disagreement over the problem of power. Political power is either, as the idealist believes, subject to a thoroughly rational process, or it is an intractable human problem requiring pragmatic and proximate checks and balances.

> The realists know that history is not a simple rational process but a vital one. All human societies are organizations of diverse vitalities and interests. Some balance of power is the basis of whatever justice is achieved in human relations. Where the disproportion of power is too great and where an equilibrium of social forces is lacking, no mere rational or moral demands can achieve justice.[36]

Realistic politics, then, takes self-interest seriously as a permanent factor in human social relations, and seeks to establish a balance of power and an equilibrium of social forces. By contrast, idealists are "inclined to view history from the standpoint of the moral and social imperatives which a rational analysis of a situation generates." The idealist looks at a problem and selects an appropriate rational response.

The argument for world government, according to Niebuhr, is an example of the idealist's tendency to seek rational solutions. A world full of conflict, say the idealists, must be replaced by a world government, a "federation of the world."

> They think of such a federation not primarily in terms of the complex economic and social interests and vitalities, which must be brought into and held in a tolerable equilibrium. Least of all do they think of the necessity of some dominant force or power as the organizing center of the equilibrium. They are on the whole content to state the ideal requirements of the situation in as rigorous terms as possible.[37]

What is implied here, of course, is that the idealist is naive in believing that if only a rational organization of the world could

---

[36]Ibid.

[37]Ibid.

somehow materialize, there no longer would be any attempts at aggression or the aggrandizement of power or wealth.

Niebuhr's biblical anthropology explodes this hope, because it presupposes that humanity will remain corrupted and egoistic until the end of history. Believing that utopia will not be established on earth until God's eschatological intervention, Niebuhr argues for "second best" solutions: the balance of power, an equilibrium of social forces, and proximate justice. It is through such a vision of the limited possibilities for justice in a fallen world that Niebuhr comes to the conclusion that a "balance of terror" between the two superpowers, armed with awesome nuclear weaponry, is the best situation one could expect given the circumstances. He even contends that this "balance of terror" will likely result in a relatively peaceful coexistence for many decades to come.[38] In this example one finds the typical Niebuhrian concession to the intractable aspects of human behavior and social organization.

There is, however, another side to the concept of realism. Realism is not only to be distinguished from idealism but also from cynicism. Niebuhr's ethic should not be interpreted as demolishing all idealism in order to relax in the knowledge that justice is unattainable. Rather, realism should be applied to the task of formulating a progressive social ethic. "A realist conception of human nature should be made the servant of an ethic of progressive justice and should not be made into a bastion of conservatism, particularly a conservatism which defends unjust privileges."[39] Niebuhr's efforts throughout his life, both as theorist and as activist, reflected this commitment to a broader and deeper justice.

In discussing Augustine's political realism, Niebuhr acknowledges the temptation of realism to become cynical if man's self-righteousness and corruption are overemphasized. "While ego-

---

[38]Reinhold Niebuhr, "Education and the World Scene," *Daedalus* 88 (Winter 1959): 117.

[39]Reinhold Niebuhr, *Man's Nature and His Communities: Essays on the Dynamics and Enigmas of Man's Personal and Social Existence* (New York: Charles Scribner's Sons, Scribner Library, 1973) 24-25.

ism is 'natural' in the sense that it is universal, it is not natural in the sense that it does not conform to man's nature who transcends himself indeterminately and can only have God rather than self for his end." Sin is inevitable but not normative. To interpret sinfulness as a norm is to take a cynical approach to human nature. "A realism becomes morally cynical or nihilistic when it assumes that the universal characteristic [of egoism] in human behavior must be regarded as normative."[40] Thus Augustine's view, the classical Christian view, escapes the errors of idealism and cynicism regarding human nature.

The distinction between realism and cynicism is not only crucial to Niebuhr's understanding of human nature; it is also essential for discerning the moral ambiguities of the social order, in both its political and economic aspects. Niebuhr observes among America's leaders three types of individuals: sentimentalists, cynics, and hypocrites. The implicit fourth type is the realist. "The sentimentalists imagine that the life of nations can be brought into conformity with the purest standards of generosity; the cynics deny every moral standard in political and economic life because they have discerned the morally ambiguous elements in it; the hypocrites profess one standard and practice another." The sentimentalists, says Niebuhr, seem reluctant to wield power because it corrupts. The cynics seem all too eager to exercise it, but without the restraints of conscience. The hypocrites pretend to the moral exercise of power, but know they are only pretending.

What is needed is an approach that avoids the extremes.

> It was one of the merits of the Christian interpretation of the human situation that it understood, as Pascal put it, both the dignity and the misery of man, both his capacity for goodness and his corruption of that goodness. It insisted that men ought to consider the rights of their fellow men; but it also knew that they never did so perfectly. It knew that human sin made coercion in government necessary; but it also knew that the lust for power of the ruler made government dangerous. It regarded all human majes-

---

[40]Niebuhr, *Christian Realism and Political Problems*, 129-30.

ties as, at the same time, derived from the divine majesty and in rebellion against it.[41]

This passage is one of the most complete expressions of the paradoxic view of the relation of the two realms to be found anywhere in Niebuhr's writings. It exemplifies a viewpoint that seeks to avoid both cynicism and sentimentalism. It is a view that takes seriously the factors of self-interest and power that offer resistance to established norms. But it does not give up the quest for higher norms and a more consistent adherence to the ideal of justice.

The distinctions among cynicism, sentimentalism, and realism are valid at all levels of reflection upon Christian ethics and political theology. They apply to the domestic and international arenas, as well as to political and economic matters. Realism recognizes "an admixture of self-seeking" in every type of human community, so it is necessary to develop political strategies for limiting the impact of this egoism upon society.

Both economic and political accumulations of power must be critically evaluated and checked. "We cannot (as does classical liberalism) regard the self-seeking which a bourgeois-liberal economy permits as completely harmless; and we cannot, as does orthodox Protestantism, particularly Lutheranism, be uncritical toward the coercive power of government on the ground that God ordained it to prevent anarchy." Neither bourgeois economic power nor coercive political power is pure in its drive toward the common good. "For both the economic power which competes in the market place and the political power which sets restraints upon the competition are tainted by motives other than the desire for justice."[42] Both the libertarian and the statist policies toward the marketplace are dangerous. Advocates of both types of policy tend to be blind to the fact that their vested self-interests are served by particular economic structures.

---

[41]Niebuhr, *Reinhold Niebuhr on Politics*, 281.

[42]Ibid., 195.

Nevertheless, there are ways to turn this self-interest to the common good.

> It would be wrong to be too cynical about this admixture of self-interest in all the vital forces of society. Men do have a residual capacity for justice. Government does express the desire of a community for order and justice; and not merely the will-to-power of the oligarchy which controls the engines of power in government. An attitude which avoids both sentimentality and cynicism must obviously be grounded in a Christian view of human nature which is schooled by the Gospel not to take the pretensions of men at their face value, on the one hand, and, on the other, not to deny the residual capacity for justice among even sinful men.[43]

Realism, then, cannot mean denying the possibility of justice; it simply avoids the overly optimistic presuppositions of the idealist or sentimentalist, and at the same time denies the overly gloomy attitude of the cynic or nihilist. Realism seeks with all its power greater justice. It is a quest with open eyes, with careful attention to tangible gains, with constant and uncompromising self-criticism. From Niebuhr's point of view, only a self-critical, non-utopian progressivism actually succeeds in increasing the quotient of justice in the real world. And nothing greater than an incremental achievement of political progress can be expected. One seeks to leave the world somewhat better than one finds it. Realism offers an alternative path to the detours of ineffective rhetoric or unprincipled action: it is neither idealistic nor cynical.

Niebuhr located the key to a progressive social ethic in a realistic and dynamic view of human nature. His concept of "realism" is not unlike Maritain's view of "practical wisdom." And, like Maritain, Niebuhr sought to tie his fundamental concept to an understanding of the virtues.

Justice and Love: Niebuhr on the Virtues

Niebuhr followed the logic of a progressive realism to the conclusion that a paradoxic blend of justice and love was fundamen-

---

[43]Ibid.

tal to politics. Indeed, D. B. Robertson writes, "The relationship between love and justice has been the major problem for Niebuhr in his elaboration of a social ethic."[44] It was also a major problem for many other Christian ethicists of Niebuhr's day. While Niebuhr sought to express an ethic that encompassed both love and justice, many other ethicists were simply choosing between them. The more liberal-minded ethicists spoke of love as the engine of a new social order. Some were Marxists, others were non-Marxist utopians. Niebuhr had a strong tendency to side with the former camp: his early "Marxian" stage illustrates this tendency. Yet he felt that he had to acknowledge the veracity of what the critics of utopianism were saying. The more conservative-minded ethicists argued that justice, not love, was the only important principle for establishing social order. Niebuhr was uncomfortable with this seemingly unavoidable choice. He sought a way to understand the importance of both love and justice.

One might assume—and many have done so—that Niebuhr's criticisms of utopian schemes of world government and unilateral disarmament mean that he finds no use for the impulse of love in the political arena. On the contrary, he argues emphatically that love is the very standard of justice in all communities, and that it is central to any Christian approach to the problems of the temporal world. Love is "a principle of discriminate criticism among various forms of community and various attempts at justice."[45] Love is, in fact, the underlying animus of a discriminating social ethic. There is a proper time and place for even the most sacrificial and ego-denying forms of love. "Even the purest form of *Agape*, the love of the enemy and forgiveness toward the evil-doer, do not stand in contradiction to historical possibilities."[46] To turn

---

[44]See Reinhold Niebuhr, *Love and Justice: Selections from the Shorter Writings of Reinhold Niebuhr*, ed. D. B. Robertson (Philadelphia: Westminster Press, 1957; rpt., Gloucester MA: Peter Smith, 1976) 9.

[45]Reinhold Niebuhr, *Christianity and Power Politics* (New York: Charles Scribner's Sons, 1940; rpt., Hamden CT: Archon Books, 1969) 26.

[46]Reinhold Niebuhr, *The Nature and Destiny of Man*, 2 vols. (New York: Charles Scribner's Sons, Scribner Library, 1941-1943) 2:85.

the other cheek, in some cases, may actually lead the aggressor to a change of heart. Nevertheless, a distinction remains between love and justice. As with Maritain's view of the two realms, Niebuhr's approach to the relationship of love and justice follows the dictum *distinguer pour unir,* "distinguish in order to unite."

In a situation of political conflict, there is a difference between sacrifice and nonresistance, on the one hand, and the search for a tolerable balance of competing interests, on the other. How can these two be reconciled?

> Perfect love is sacrificial love, making no careful calculations between the interests of self and the other. Perfect justice is discriminating and calculating, carefully measuring the limits of interests and the relation between the interests of the self and the other. . . . What can this heedlessness of *Agape* have to do with discrimination?
>
> The love which is the final criterion is obviously a principle of criticism upon all political and economic realities, since it reveals the sinful element of self-seeking and of coercive restraint in all forms of human community. But does it help us to arrive at discriminate choices among alternative systems and policies, since all them have morally ambiguous elements in them?[47]

Niebuhr answers his own question by identifying love with the principle of self-criticism. He focuses on the gospel-inspired realization that all temporal and human realities are utterly limited in the face of the radically Other, the righteous God. "The heedlessness of love, which sacrifices the interests of the self, enters into calculations of justice principally by becoming the spirit of contrition which issues from the self's encounter with God." Love is precisely what animates the quest for justice because it calls into question the uncritical egoism toward which all humanity tends. "This contrition is the socially relevant counterpart of love. It breaks the pride of the implacable contestants and competitors in all human encounters." Perfect love, is, indeed, sacrificial action; but it is also contrition. And contrition lays the foundation for the justice that weighs all interests and seeks a tolerable balance of

---

[47]Niebuhr, *Reinhold Niebuhr on Politics,* 157.

competing claims. Contrition is the first step toward a democratic-pluralist civic consciousness. "This spirit lies at the foundation of what we define as democracy. For democracy cannot exist if there is no recognition of the fragmentary character of all systems of thought and value which are allowed to exist together within a democratic frame."[48]

A democratic-pluralist society is not the Kingdom of God. It is a society of proximate justice. Its justice is, nevertheless, infused with the drive toward perfect love that is symbolized by the Kingdom of God. Niebuhr continually applied this realistic and progressive social ethic to the problems of his day and his community. Some of the details of his application of these principles will be explored later in a discussion of the content of Niebuhr's political philosophy.[49] For the present, it is sufficient to note that "realism" for Niebuhr implies a paradoxic or dialectical embodiment of justice and love in the political order.

All historical instances of proximate justice or balance of power are subject to the call to higher justice represented by the love commandment of Jesus. "Beyond and above every human relation as ordered by a fixed structure of justice, by custom, tradition, and legal enactment, there remain indeterminate possibilities of love in the individual and personal encounters of those who are in the structure." Love can be realized at the level of interpersonal relations, and this love can affect social structures. "Human actions can, to a degree, corrupt even the highest structure and they can also partially redeem the worst structure."[50] Love remains beyond justice. Thus Niebuhr persistently argues that, paradoxically, love is both the fulfillment and the denial of justice.

How can love both affirm and negate justice? Niebuhr answers this question by examining both *remedial* justice and *distributive* justice. If reason looks deeply into the inner sources of an evil act, it will see that neither the criminal nor the victim is entirely free

---

[48]Ibid., 158.

[49]See ch. 4.

[50]Niebuhr, *Christian Realism and Political Problems*, 167-68.

from the taint of sin; this may lead to greater justice. "But if it should become so sensitive as to recognize that the evil in the other has its sources in the self or the self's society, it will destroy every form of remedial justice." When the self becomes too contrite, it will hesitate to punish the evil act of the other. The same is true for distributive justice. "An imaginative regard for the interests of my neighbor will be concerned for his needs even if they are in competition with mine." Again, the principle of self-criticism allows a person truly to understand the interests of a neighbor, even when they are in conflict with his own. But while individuals may occasionally forfeit their own just desserts for the sake of another, this cannot be the general rule. "Such an imaginative concern for the neighbor's interests transcends all ordinary conceptions of equity and enjoins actions of generosity which no society can ever enjoin or regularize."[51]

Thus we reach an unresolvable dilemma: justice can never be equated with love; love is always "beyond."

> In so far as justice admits the claim of the self, it is something less than love. Yet it cannot exist without love and remain justice. For without the "grace" of love, justice always degenerates into something less than justice.[52]

Conversely, insofar as justice forfeits the claim of the self, it ceases to be justice and becomes sacrificial love.

Justice and love are the fruits of realism in politics. They are dialectically related in the same way that the temporal world, at its best, remains under the judgment of a perfect higher realm. To deny the higher realm is the error of the cynic. To imagine that the higher realm is simply the end result of the progress made in the temporal world of politics is the error of the utopian. For Niebuhr, the true significance of both justice and love is retained only when their distinction *and* unity are understood.

> We must recognize how dialectically the Kingdom of God is related to the sinful world in every moment of existence, offering

---

[51]Niebuhr, *Reinhold Niebuhr on Politics*, 164-65.

[52]Ibid., 165.

both judgment and a more excellent way in consideration of every problem of justice. The gospel command of love is surely in the realm of the Kingdom of God. But the Kingdom of God is not simply trans-historical. It is involved in every moment of history. It is a clue to the fact that every moment of history is a moment of judgment. . . . The love commandment is, in short, immediately relevant to every moral action.[53]

Love is relevant to politics. The best public policy aims at a proximate justice infused with the drive for a progressively deeper fulfillment of the love commandment. In this way, a political realism emerges that is effective in the real world of conflicting interests, while remaining dedicated to the higher goal of altruistic and self-limiting actions. True realism is embodied in the virtues of justice and love held in creative tension.

Niebuhr's concept of realism and Maritain's concept of practical wisdom provided each of them with an interpretative technique for formulating their political theologies. These concepts were also significant for their interpretations of the historical roots of political theology, and for their understanding of the practical details of social order.

---

[53]Ibid., 162.

TRADITIONAL SOURCES
OF CHRISTIAN POLITICAL THEORY

The diversity of the influences which entered into a politics of justice must serve to remind us that only a great multitude of diverse, and sometimes contradictory, traditions can serve to illumine the meaning and mystery of human existence.

Reinhold Niebuhr
Man's Nature and His Communities[1]

---

[1](New York: Charles Scribner's Sons, 1965) 27.

III

Every political philosophy must necessarily sink its roots in a particular historical soil. There are as many distinct political philosophies as there are cultures. Each appeals to universal values, such as justice, equality, and freedom. Yet each is set in a unique and particular cultural context. The political philosophies of Jacques Maritain and Reinhold Niebuhr are set in the context of the entire heritage of Western civilization, which blends ancient Hebrew, Greek, and Roman ideas and practices, and augments them with the contributions of various other cultures. The political philosophies of Maritain and Niebuhr are also influenced, to an especially significant degree, by the emergence of the modern democratic society. The modern Western experience of a developing pattern of limited sovereignty, representative government, pluralism, and tolerance has profoundly affected contemporary Christian political theory. Political theology can and should take account of these modern developments while remaining loyal to ancient ideals of the just society. It is precisely this task that Maritain and Niebuhr each accomplish in their own unique ways and for their own particular confessional strands of Christianity.

The phrase "democratic pluralism and human rights," which summarizes the content of the political theology of both Maritain and Niebuhr, is a peculiarly modern expression of the perennial ideal of justice. Christian thought always calls society to justice. Christian political theology expounds the conditions for a just society—or at least one that approximates the ideal.

Maritain and Niebuhr give concrete meaning to the phrase "democratic pluralism and human rights." They define the structure of the social system that is named by this phrase, and they detail its impact upon the personal and collective lives of its members. They forge a "concrete historical ideal" for social and political life.[2] Their appeals to justice, love, and prudence,which may seem to have an abstract, formal, and universalistic tenor, actually have a concrete, contingent, and historical focus: the history of Western civilization and of the democratic tradition.

Niebuhr and Maritain were historians as well as philosophers. Their images of the free society are thus both practical and theoretical. Their ideas of social order, for example, are derived not only from the logical imperatives of dialectical reasoning, but also from the historical experience of the Western world. Their philosophies are based on living history, the history of Christian political theory.

The historical experience of Christianity in the Western world encompasses a broad range of intellectual traditions. As Christian theologians, Maritain and Niebuhr spoke out of particular subsets of that world—Maritain from the Thomist tradition, Niebuhr from a combination of Lutheran and Reformed traditions that characterized the small Evangelical Reformed church in which he was nurtured and ordained. Yet both Maritain and Niebuhr were theologians to the larger church. Beginning with the biblical kerygma, each drew insights from one tradition or another to construct a political theology for the universal church.

---

[2]This is a favorite phrase of Maritain's; see his *Integral Humanism: Temporal and Spiritual Problems of a New Christendom*, trans. Joseph W. Evans (New York: Charles Scribner's Sons, 1968; rpt., Notre Dame IN: University of Notre Dame Press, 1973) ch. 4.

In addition, both Maritain and Niebuhr went beyond the legacy of Christian thought to include the insights of Greek, Roman, and modern secular philosophers. Thomism, for example, is greatly dependent upon its Aristotelian base, while the Protestant tradition owes much to Augustinianism. Both traditions are indebted to Greco-Roman Stoicism for the notion of natural law and the subsequent formulation of the doctrine of the two realms. Niebuhr and Maritain also surveyed the thought of modern theologians for possible additions to the political theology of justice and freedom.

In each area of historical scholarship, there are treasures of insight to be discovered and assimilated to the essentially Hebraic perspective of the Scriptures. Ultimately, the ancient quest for justice and freedom must be translated into a search for modern forms of democratic pluralism and respect for fundamental human rights. The political theologies that result from this search for roots are rightly understood as both traditional and modern, in the best sense of both words.

The Doctrine of the Two Realms in Christian Political Theology

The major issue in the history of Christian political theology is the proper relationship of religion and politics. There are other themes too, but how Christians have understood and symbolized this relationship is crucial, because religion and politics are the domains of humanity's most cherished spiritual and temporal values. Ever since Jesus' command to "Render therefore to Caesar the things that are Caesar's, and to God the things that are God's" (Matt. 22:21), indeed long before that, men and women have pondered the question of the relationship of religion and politics.

In that statement Jesus was expressing, among other things, a sense of the inviolability—even the sacredness—of conscience. Christianity teaches that, in an ultimate sense, some things are more important than obedience to the government. Conscience and the life of the spirit have priority over the demands of society. Furthermore, a theistic humanism in the modern era establishes institutional safeguards for the freedom of conscience and dignity of individuals.

In Christian thought this problem is addressed by the doctrine of the two realms. God and man, heaven and earth, spiritual and material, eternal and temporal, sacred and secular, religion and politics, church and state—running through each of these pairs is an intuition of two basic orders of reality with two corresponding realms of authority or two aspects of the same authority. In the early days of the Christian faith, when Peter and the other apostles were commanded by the authorities to cease preaching in the name of Jesus, they replied, "We must obey God rather than men" (Acts 5:29). They did not deny the legitimacy of human laws. They were not anarchists cynically using spiritual rhetoric. Rather, they were expressing a sense of dual obligation: their duty to obey the ruler, and their higher duty to obey God.[3]

Reinhold Niebuhr echoes this dual obligation of the Christian and offers some advice for Christians and others when he suggests that every concerned citizen should have both a "critical attitude" and a "responsible attitude" toward every type of political society and government.[4] How these two obligations come together in a perfect harmony is summarized by Maritain in his 1927 essay, La Primauté du Spirituel: "A Christian political order in the world . . . is a fruit produced by the spirit of faith." The ideal, for Maritain, does not come about artificially; it is produced through heartfelt commitment. "It presupposes a living and practical faith in a large number of people, a civilization inspired by Christian wisdom, an over-all orientation of political life towards the true goods of the person and of the spirit. We are far from this ideal."[5]

---

[3]Compare the Apostle Paul's own view of the "dual obligation" in the section "Maritain and Niebuhr on Paul's 'Powers That Be.' "

[4]Niebuhr's extended comment on the "critical attitude" and the "responsible attitude" is quoted in the section "Key Interpretative Concepts" in ch. 2.

[5]Jacques Maritain, The Social and Political Philosophy of Jacques Maritain: Selected Readings, ed. Joseph W. Evans and Leo R. Ward (New York: Charles Scribner's Sons, 1955; rpt., Notre Dame IN: University of Notre Dame Press, 1976) 145-46.

How do Maritain and Niebuhr understand the relationship of religion and politics? As a preliminary answer to the question, one might say that the relation is one of *creative tension*. It is clear that for Christianity there are two orders of authority, that these orders impinge on each other in each of our lives, and that certain distinctions are necessary with regard to the commingled presence of religion and politics in the social fabric of life.

The fundamental concept that governs the ideas of both Maritain and Niebuhr, the doctrine of the two realms, is founded upon a biblical view of reality and certain extrabiblical concepts that have been assimilated to the Christian tradition. Consonant with the typical biblical tension, the doctrine of the two realms suggests that Christ and culture are distinct, but that they are related through an eschatologically transformative process. Thus political authority is grounded in humanity but judged and redeemed by divinity. Christianity's distinction between natural law and divine law is the very basis of its antipathy toward every form of political absolutism.

Maritain and Niebuhr agree that at the heart of the heritage of Christian political theology is an ethos built upon the doctrines of selfhood, love, and the Kingdom of God. The doctrine of *selfhood* asserts the unity and freedom of the individual, the fulfillment of self through love of the other, and the corruption of freedom through self-love. These are the existentialist, humanist, and realist contributions to the idea of selfhood. The doctrine of *love* establishes divine *agape*—mercy, self-giving love—as the ideal standard for human action. This is the virtue of charity, which infuses the social order through equal respect for all individuals and mutual participation in society. The *Kingdom of God* symbolizes the end or purpose of social existence, the continual transformation of culture by Spirit. Thus nature and history are intrinsically good and ultimately redeemable.

Finally, how did Maritain and Niebuhr see the relationship of natural law to divine law? While there are some differences between them on this issue, a common ground underlies their differences. The tradition of practical wisdom or realism is based on the fundamental notion of truth. Truth is the gift of God and the goal toward which human virtue is directed. Political society is established and perfected through the exercise of practical wisdom. The Christian world view presupposes the idea of a natural law—an unwritten law, order, or disposition which human reason can discover and to which the human will should conform. The natural law is not an extrinsic or a priori plan in nature that dictates all moral decisions. On the contrary, natural law is an intrinsic reality in the depths of a human person, who is a free and responsible moral agent. Natural law requires that actions be aimed at the true common good of political society. Practical wisdom, then, is the exercise of conscience dedicated to making the truth of God and the God-centeredness of the world the measure for will and action. Practical wisdom or prudence is the mother of the temporal virtues just as charity is the first theological virtue. Both prudence and charity are human virtues infused by divine grace and focused on seeking the good of the neighbor in every sphere.

The ancient philosophical understanding of lex naturalis was apprehended in different ways by theologians throughout history. Maritain and Niebuhr devoted considerable attention to this problem through the course of their careers. They concluded that, whereas universal human reason teaches that right government is truth-in-action aimed at the good, Christianity adds that true justice entails a proper relationship of the two realms. Christianity gives natural law a distinct theological depth by emphasizing sin, salvation, and the Kingdom of God. The end result is an ethic of responsibility.

Maritain and Niebuhr on Paul's "Powers that Be"

A comparison of Maritain and Niebuhr yields indirect evidence of their compatibility in the ways they handle certain elements of their common Christian tradition. How did they understand, for example, the well-known biblical passage in which the Apostle Paul refers to the "governing authorities"? In the passage Paul seems to make a case, in Christian terms, for the legitimacy of political authority under certain conditions. Paul writes,

Let every person be subject to the governing authorities. For there is no authority except for God, and those that exist have been instituted by God. Therefore he who resists the authorities resists what God has appointed, and those who resist will incur judgment. For rulers are not a terror to good conduct, but to bad. Would you have no fear of him who is in authority? Then do what is good, and you will receive his approval, for he is God's servant for your good. But if you do wrong, be afraid, for he does not bear the sword in vain; he is the servant of God to execute his wrath on the wrongdoer. Therefore one must be subject, not only to avoid God's wrath but also for the sake of conscience. For the same reason you also pay taxes, for the authorities are ministers of God, attending to this very thing. Pay all of them their dues, taxes to whom taxes are due, revenue to whom revenue is due, respect to whom respect is due, honor to whom honor is due.

Owe no one anything, except to love one another; for he who loves his neighbor has fulfilled the law (Rom. 13:1-8).

Paul had been the chief persecutor of Christians. After his conversion he dedicated his life to proclaiming the good news of Christ and the mystery of an evil world already somehow participating in its own future redemption. All men, said Paul, have a perception of God and God's will through a natural law. "When Gentiles who have not the law *do by nature* what the law requires, they are a law unto themselves" (Rom. 2:14, emphasis added). The Christian, argued Paul, is free from the religious law; because he lives its spirit, he is no longer in need of its letter. Likewise, as a citizen of a political community, the Christian will give no offense to anyone and accept all legitimate responsibilities. He will give "taxes to whom taxes are due . . . honor to whom honor is due" (Rom. 13:7).

Paul believed that rulers wield their power legitimately when they truly serve the common good. Both Maritain and Niebuhr argue that Paul's admonition does not give carte blanche to the ruler. Rather, the authorities must only be obeyed when obedience is "their due."

Maritain interprets the passage as a clear statement that political power is not divine but earthly. While it may serve a godly purpose, it is not God. Its majesty rests only in the fact that it represents the common will of the people.

> The civil power bears the impress of majesty: this is not because it represents God. It is because it represents the people, the whole multitude and its common will to live together. And by the same token since it represents the people, the civil power holds its authority through the people, from the Primary Cause of Nature and of human society. [And in a sense—a theologian would add—from Christ's universal kingship. But this no more makes him a representative of Christ than an image of God.] St. Paul teaches that "there is no authority that is not from God" and that those who bear the sword are "God's ministers" or "functionaries of God," "appointed by God" (let us understand, through the people) "to inflict his wrathful vengeance upon him that doth wrong." Never did he teach that they were the image of God. What essentially constituted, in its own temporal or political order, the majesty of the king is the same as what the majesty of the President of a democratic nation consists of.[6]

Thus Paul's admonition to the Christian to obey political authorities when obedience is due cannot be construed as a defense of political absolutism or the status quo. There remain two distinct realms of authority in vital relationship to one another. God's authority is supreme over all, but the authority of one who rules with the consent of the people is relatively autonomous in its own sphere.

Similarly, Niebuhr interprets Paul's admonition as a legitimation of political authority that is properly constituted. Niebuhr emphasizes, in contrast to Maritain, the tension between the "realistic mood" expressed by this passage and the "idealistic mood" that appears elsewhere in Paul's writings.

> In his idealistic moods, Paul made perfect love (*Agape*, the love of God for man) into the new and higher standard of the "new Israel," the redeemed community, the church, which was the "body of Christ" (I Cor. 12:13). In his realistic moods, he con-

---

[6]Jacques Maritain, *Man and the State* (Chicago: University of Chicago Press, Phoenix Books, 1951) 131. The sentences in brackets are contained in a footnote.

ceded that the new community would have to deal with a morally ambiguous human nature and civil society must have the higher "authority" from God "to execute his wrath on the wrongdoer," to "restrain the evil," this higher authority being "instituted by God" (Rom. 13:1, 4). This realistic sanctification of civil authority was to be fatefully used, particularly by the Reformation, to induce an uncritical reverence for established authority, however unjust.[7]

Here and elsewhere Niebuhr makes it clear that Paul's statement cannot be used to divinize any ruler or policy. Niebuhr clearly supports the right of resistance to established authority in the extreme case in which the ruler no longer truly represents the people. He notes that certain theologians, like Luther and Calvin, have insisted on obedience even to unjust rulers, but he maintains that Paul could not have intended his words to be interpreted in this way.

Maritain and Niebuhr understand Paul's teaching to consist of a qualified assent to the authority of the ruler. The stated and implied qualification is that the ruler must be a genuine representative of the people and must truly act in the interest of the common good. Ideally, the ruler will be democratically elected. If these conditions are met, the ruler may legitimately inflict punishment on the criminal, wage war against an enemy, collect taxes, and otherwise properly exercise his power. Yet, by legitimating the actions of the just ruler, Christianity does not sacralize his policies. There is no confusion of the two realms. The sacred and secular realms remain distinct, each with its own autonomy in relation to the other. Furthermore, the necessity for political authority is connected with the natural order. For Maritain, this means that a natural law underlies all human reality. For Niebuhr, politics is "natural" only in the sense that it reflects, in its morally ambiguous character, the universality of human conflict and sinfulness. For both Maritain and Niebuhr, Christ commands obedience to legitimately constituted political authority.

---

[7]Niebuhr, *Man's Nature and His Communities*, 42-43.

Maritain and Niebuhr on Augustine's "Two Cities"

One of the greatest of the church fathers, Augustine, echoed the Pauline vision of a natural law to which government should conform and added the realistic acknowledgment that the state is a "fallen" or sin-infected institution. Augustine viewed the *civitas* as imperfect and incomplete. Both Maritain and Niebuhr rely heavily on the insights of Augustine as they elaborate their political theologies. As with Paul, they find in Augustine a clear distinction between the sacred and secular realms accompanied by a genuine concern that justice be established in the temporal realm.

In *The Structure of Nations and Empires*, Niebuhr assesses Augustine's contribution to political theology. Augustine had adopted, according to Niebuhr, the Stoic conception of a cosmic order transcending particular social orders. Augustine used the concepts of the "City of God" and the "City of the World" to express the "tension between universalism and imperialism," a tension that had troubled both the Stoics and the Roman emperors. Yet Augustine thought the two cities were "more incompatible" than did the Stoics.[8]

The concept of the two cities became a central theme spurring medieval efforts to create a new civilization based on the Christian model. Augustine and later thinkers assumed "a 'commingling' of the two cities, the heavenly acting as a leaven for the earthly city by drawing it from its proximate ends to the ultimate end."[9] Niebuhr criticizes the "utopian" qualities of Augustine's conception of the ideal community, but he notes that by this device Augustine was able to give a realistic account of the successes and failures of historical cities, to point out their merely proximate forms of justice. "If Augustine's description of the *civ-*

---

[8]Reinhold Niebuhr, *The Structure of Nations and Empires: A Study of the Recurring Patterns and Problems of the Political Order in Relation to the Unique Problems of the Nuclear Age* (New York: Charles Scribner's Sons, 1959; rpt., Fairfield NJ: Augustus H. Kelley, 1977) 84.

[9]Ibid., 102.

itas dei is remarkably 'utopian' and bears little relation to any known reality, yet it is by the perspective of this illusion that he can give such a realistic account of the *civitas terrena*, or of any community in history."[10]

For Niebuhr, Augustine's great contribution to Christian political theory was his vivid description of the two realms, of which the lower achieved only a proximate order and justice. The state, in Augustine's view, is both the result of sin and the remedy for sin. It addresses the problem of the inevitable clash of selfish interests, but it will ultimately be transformed into a "City of God" at the end of history.

Maritain also acknowledges the significance of Augustine's thought, particularly his clear delineation of the two realms. Maritain agrees with Niebuhr that Augustine emphasizes the *differences* rather than the *similarities* between the two realms. There is no automatic or simple compatibility between the two cities; rather, there can only be a dynamic historical and transhistorical process by which the norms of the heavenly city impinge upon the practices of the earthly city. No final solution of the tension is possible until the end of history. Maritain concludes that the Augustinian view of politics is more realistic than many other views—including that of Aristotle, for example.

Maritain finds Aristotelian political theory too idealistic. Its more mechanistic and rationalistic view of the *civitas* does not achieve the level of realism exemplified by Augustine. "A genuine temporal community of mankind [is] not the perfect *civitas* in the Aristotelian sense, but that kind of *civitas* in the Augustinian sense, which is imperfect and incomplete, made up of a fluid network of human communications, and more existential than formally organized, but all the more real and living and basically important."[11] Maritain's comment on Augustine's idea of the *civitas* illustrates his dynamic view of natural law. The earthly city does conform to certain rational and natural parameters of human existence. Yet it is not as fixed and unchanging as, for example,

---

[10]Ibid., 105.

[11]Maritain, *The Social and Political Philosophy of Jacques Maritain*, 319.

the law of gravity. Natural law changes as human beings change. Politics progresses or regresses according to the free choices of real human beings. Political progress, if it happens at all, is *existential*, not mechanistic.

Once again, Maritain and Niebuhr differ on their precise understandings of natural law, but they agree that Augustine's contribution to political theology is immeasurable. Augustine clearly separates the two realms, and he dramatically asserts the divine, eschatological conversion of the secular realm by the sacred realm.

Maritain and Niebuhr on Aquinas's "Natural Law"

The differences between Maritain and Niebuhr are perhaps most clearly seen in their respective treatments of Thomism and the Catholic notion of natural law. In a sense, both men testify to the power of the concept of natural law. The concept has allowed Western culture to locate the rationale for politics in reason itself. To Maritain, this concept of natural law, properly understood, *does not* obscure the nonrational qualities that human beings bring to their political existence. To Niebuhr, natural law *does* overemphasize man's capacity for reason and thus masks the nonrational and truly dialectical nature of the political realm. Neither Maritain nor Niebuhr disputes the importance or the power of the idea of natural law; they disagree on whether the doctrine is sufficient—in and of itself—to reveal the truth about the secular realm.

Thomas Aquinas synthesized in his political thought the various insights of Greco-Roman philosophy and Christian theology that he inherited from earlier thinkers. He achieved this grand synthesis of Christian social teachings by utilizing the principle of natural law crowned by the doctrine of redemption. Aquinas perceived a continuity between human and religious values. Grace perfects nature. Sin is a human reality, but sin does not obliterate the natural, ethical values revealed by reason. Thus man is responsible for establishing justice that will render to each person his due, his natural rights. Politics and the state are tools in this task. Like Aristotle, Aquinas locates the rationale for the state directly in the nature of man. He interprets Aristotle's ideal form of government, or "polity," as a limited monarchy in which authority descends through a metaphysical hierarchy from God to the ruler, to the law, and to the people. Aquinas advocates a monarchy responsible to the people and truly reflective of the higher realm of divine justice. He argues that the essence of law is reason, in contrast to later thinkers, such as Marsilius and Machiavelli, who grounded law in power.

Maritain takes great care to point out the error of those commentators who see Thomas Aquinas as an apologist for unlimited sovereignty. Maritain teaches that, for Aquinas, the state cannot claim a sacred status, nor can the ruler abuse the trust that he has from God and the people to seek the common good. Maritain argues that the idea of man in the metaphysics of Aristotle and Thomas Aquinas is "the rational foundation of democratic philosophy."[12]

> The organs of government are then regarded by the Christian as having in God, as does any legitimate power, the source of their authority, yet as not taking on, even by participation, a sacred character. Once the organs are designated, authority resides in them, but in virtue of a certain consensus, of a free and vital determination made by the people, whose personification and vicar they are: vices gerens multitudinus, as St. Thomas puts it.[13]

Thomistic political philosophy is founded on an ethic of responsibility that ought to be manifested by both the ruler and subject. "If the aim of politics is the common good," Maritain writes, "the ruler, having to take care of the temporal end of a community of human persons, . . . must learn to be, as St. Thomas taught, a man good in every respect." By contrast, a political ethic that eschews responsibility is at war with the good. Maritain continues, "If the aim of politics is power, the ruler must learn not to be good, as Machiavelli said."[14]

Thus Aquinas prefigures an emerging democratic mentality, which grounds political authority in popular consensus, and

---

[12]Ibid., 121.

[13]Maritain, Integral Humanism, 200.

[14]Maritain, The Social and Political Philosophy of Jacques Maritain, 302.

which establishes a regime dedicated to the pursuit of the virtues of prudence, justice, and charity. Once again, Christian political theology emphasizes the distinction between the two realms and judges the political order in terms of the transcendent standard of justice. On this point, as with all matters of substance, Maritain and Aquinas are in complete agreement.

Niebuhr also shares with Maritain and Aquinas this basic two-realms doctrine. However, he takes Aquinas as an example of the excesses of rationalism and a mechanistic cosmology. Niebuhr writes, "The errors of natural law theory find expression in an unwarranted confidence in human reason."[15] Perhaps Niebuhr does not see in Aquinas's work what Maritain sees; namely, the important balancing of the ideas of reason and caritas. Niebuhr does clearly see what he believes is an inordinate faith in reason.

> The perennial mistake of rationalists, whether Stoic, Catholic or modern, is to exempt reason from either finiteness or sin or both, and to derive universal rational norms for this confidence in reason. This mistake may be remedied by a more dialectical analysis of the function of reason. Reason is in fact in an equivocal position between the self-as-subject and the self-as-agent of action, between the self as transcending itself and the anxious self in action. It is the servant of both.[16]

Niebuhr believes this overly rationalistic approach obscures our understanding of politics. "Natural law theories which derive absolutely valid principles of morals and politics from reason invariably introduce contingent practical applications into the definitions of principles."[17] Natural law never lives up to its promise of objectivity; according to Niebuhr, it always manifests its historicity.

Thomistic definitions of justice are filled with specific details

---

[15]Reinhold Niebuhr, *Reinhold Niebuhr on Politics: His Political Philosophy and Its Application to Our Age as Expressed in His Writings*, ed. Harry R. Davis and Robert C. Good (New York: Charles Scribner's Sons, 1960) 170.

[16]Ibid.

[17]Ibid., 170-71.

which are drawn from the given realities of a feudal social order and may be regarded as "rationalizations" of a feudal aristocracy's dominant position in society. Bourgeois idealists of the eighteenth century invented new natural law theories and invested them with bourgeois rather than feudal-aristocratic content.[18]

In spite of his rather harsh criticisms of natural law theory (and, by implication, of Aquinas and Maritain), Niebuhr understood the positive but limited truth in the idea of natural law.

While it is important to reject the errors of the natural law theorists, it is just as important to disavow the opposite error of the moral relativists, who deny every validity of general norms.

The fact is that there are some general principles of justice which define the right order of life in a community. There are no living communities which do not have some notions of justice beyond their historic laws, by which they seek to gauge the justice of their legislative enactments.[19]

Niebuhr concludes by arguing that natural law—rightly understood—is not rationalism but rather a rational effort to fulfill the love commandment.

The principles of natural law by which justice is defined are, however, not so much fixed standards of reason as they are rational efforts to apply the moral obligation implied in the love commandment to the complexities of life and the fact of sin; that is, to the situation created by the inclination of men to take advantage of each other.[20]

Aquinas and Maritain can be vindicated, then, from Niebuhr's point of view since they conceive of the natural law as dynamic and dialectical. Niebuhr and Maritain may, in fact, not be so far apart on this issue as they at first appear. Niebuhr's attempt to show the intertwined goals of reason and love may somehow

---

[18]Ibid.

[19]Ibid., 172-73.

[20]Ibid., 173.

dimly reflect the balance between natural law and *caritas* in Aquinas's thought.

Maritain and Niebuhr on Luther's "Two Swords"

A reversal of roles for Maritain and Niebuhr occurs in moving from Aquinas to Luther. Here Maritain is quite critical, while Niebuhr is much less so. It must be understood that Maritain's comments about Luther in *Three Reformers* came about through a special set of circumstances. He began writing about Luther during World War I and, according to some scholars,[21] used his writing at that time as a vehicle for a critique of German aggression. By the time of the appearance of *True Humanism* (1936), Maritain was writing about Luther in more appreciative terms, acknowledging his historical contributions even while rejecting his "errors."

Nevertheless, Maritain's comments about Luther in *Three Reformers* are revealing. The book is an acerbic polemic against Luther, Descartes, and Rousseau; together, according to Maritain, they are responsible for the rise of an ill-founded *individualism* that replaced the traditional *personalism* of Christianity. Luther, in particular, is seen as the source of a certain anti-intellectual subjectivism or fideism at odds with the ancient metaphysics that asserted the harmony of faith and reason. "It is Jean-Jacques [Rousseau] who completed this unheard-of operation begun by Luther of inventing a Christianity separated from the Church of Christ."[22]

Granted that Maritain's primary disagreement with Luther is one of metaphysics, it is important to recognize within this issue a political disagreement. Luther's subjectivism, according to Maritain, leads to an un-Christian cynicism about the world and the political order. His two-swords doctrine too radically separates the secular realm from divine grace.

---

[21]See, for example, William J. Nottingham, *Christian Faith and Secular Action* (St. Louis: Bethany Press, 1968) 52.

[22]Jacques Maritain, *Trois Réformateurs* (Paris: Librairie Plon, 1925) 211; quoted ibid., 53.

[This error] consists in making of the world and of the earthly city purely and simply the kingdom of Satan, the domain solely of the devil. Their whole history is turned in a direction opposite to that of the Church and tends to the kingdom of perdition. It is what we may call a *satanocratic* conception of the world and of the political city. This conception acquired a certain doctrinal force at the time of the Protestant Reformation.[23]

Elsewhere Maritain criticizes "the immanentist conception of conscience which, since the Lutheran revolution, has little by little prevailed, and which asks of what is in man, of 'my interior freedom,' that it alone construct morality for itself, without any indebtedness to law."[24] Thus, it is clear that Maritain believes that democracy and human rights are not easily maintained or defended on the philosophic ground of Luther's thought; an immanentism that denies transcendence and a subjectivism that denies reason cannot sustain the "new Christendom." The two-swords doctrine—originally a Catholic notion—had become in Luther's hands a doctrine destined to be used to sacralize all manner of evil.

Niebuhr is much less critical of Luther; yet he *is* critical on precisely the same issue. Luther's ideas, according to Niebuhr, too neatly separated the earthly sphere from the heavenly sphere and allowed injustice to masquerade as the secular expression of God's will. Luther, like Augustine, saw the earthly city as that order which is maintained by coercion and force. But, says Niebuhr, Luther's conception "lacks the expansive dimensions of Augustine's *civitas terrena.*"[25]

It is, in fact, simply defined as *obrigkeit,* or authority. The imperial authority is vaguely in the background, but the relevant authority is the princely elector, who became Luther's protector. Luther does not concern himself with the problem of a universal order, but only with the order in the parochial community of his experience. In that community order is maintained by coercive

---

[23]Maritain, *Integral Humanism,* 103.

[24]Maritain, *The Social and Political Philosophy of Jacques Maritain,* 23.

[25]Niebuhr, *The Structure of Nations and Empires,* 143.

authority; and Augustine's conception of a relative justice, derived from the balance of social forces, disappears.[26]

In Niebuhr's view, Luther was right to have challenged over-
whelming papal authority, to have rejected the sentimentality of
a quasiuniversal empire, and to have recognized the place of coercive authority in maintaining any political order. Unfortunately,
Luther went on to produce "an uncritical political absolutism and
particularism."

Niebuhr concludes his discussion of Luther in The Structure
of Nations and Empires by noting that one of the chief remaining
tasks of political realism is to put itself back into the service of
justice.[27] Having rejected sentimental schemes of justice, realists
are obligated to formulate alternative strategies by which justice
can be expanded. This, Niebuhr believed, was not possible on the
basis of Luther's thought alone. Still, Niebuhr felt that there were
many positive results from Luther's work and the Reformation in
general.

Whereas the Roman Catholic tradition of natural law and
practical wisdom concentrated on apprehending God as Truth in
nature, Protestantism shifted its attention to proclaiming God as
Goodness in history. Of course, God is beyond both nature and
history, but his manifestations are to be found in the visible world.
God's dynamic and active power, rather than his eternal perfection, was the focus of the Protestant reformers. Such generaliza-
tions do not represent exclusive categories of thought for Roman
Catholicism and Protestantism. They do suggest, however, certain distinctive styles. Both traditions emphasize the importance
of society's "orders"—church, state, family, work, and so forth. But
whereas Roman Catholicism viewed God's sovereignty over the
orders of society as hierarchical, Protestantism asserted God's direct and immediate sovereignty over each order of society. Therefore, Roman Catholicism places political obligation within a
context of the interconnected duties of individual Christians.

---

[26]Ibid.

[27]Ibid., 144.

Protestantism, on the other hand, establishes a distinct and separate status for political obligation, according to the legitimacy of the order of civil government, and holds it in paradoxical relation to the other orders and their corresponding obligations. Protestantism has accordingly emphasized the necessity of checks and balances between orders, between ruler and ruled, between obligations to church, state, family, and work.

For Luther, the state is a necessary restraint upon evil in a world that God mysteriously allows to remain fallen. The Christian citizen is free from the law, yet obligated to a deeper law of love for God and neighbor. The two realms are not related hierarchically or analogically, only paradoxically, in the same way that law and gospel are related. The heavenly realm both fulfills and abrogates the earthly realm.

In spite of the dangers of political parochialism and ethical privatism, Luther's view of the relation of religion and politics is an example of realism with regard to power. This is essential to a viable Christian political theology. The world is fallen and corrupt. Justice is achieved only partially and through an unfortunate and unsavory coercion.

Luther retained many medieval ideas of justice, including equity and natural law. He argued that, in the ideal case, the ruler is a servant of God's justice, using coercion, but perfecting it by the leaven of reason, and perfecting reason by love. The citizen has a dual obligation to respect the authorities of the two realms. His vocation is full participation in civil life, and it parallels his election to spiritual life.

The Christian cannot withdraw from participation in civil affairs, however unpleasant and inconsistent they are with his ultimate hope. But he can bring justice and love to fruition in the earthly realm. The key to Luther's ethic is personal responsibility. When exaggerated, however, personal responsibility leads to an un-Christian individualism and privatization of ethics and faith.

Both Maritain and Niebuhr criticize Luther for elaborating a two-swords doctrine that allowed too much freedom to the secular sphere. Both are concerned about the way political absolutism arose in a "Lutheran" atmosphere—for example, in Luther's own time with the Peasant's Revolt and, in later times, with Hitler's Nazism. Yet Niebuhr, unlike Maritain, more readily rejects the pre-Lutheran "medieval synthesis" as a model for the just society. Nevertheless, the degree to which Maritain and Niebuhr are in relative agreement comes through implicitly in their treatments of Luther.

Indeed, the basic consonance of thought between Maritain and Niebuhr is evident in their treatments of Paul, Augustine, Aquinas, and Luther. In each case—and down through the centuries of Christian thought—the paradox of separate but correlative authorities has been the primary datum of political theology, and the Christian doctrine of the two realms has provided the categories for interpreting the paradox. Such an assessment of the contributions of these four major thinkers, along with scores of other historically significant theologians, is a crucial task for our times. It is a prerequisite to the emergence of a truly ecumenical political theology.

DEMOCRATIC PLURALISM
AND HUMAN RIGHTS

The American Constitution . . . is deep-rooted in the age-old heritage of Christian thought and civilization. . . . The Founding Fathers were neither metaphysicians nor theologians, but their philosophy of life, and their political philosophy, their notion of natural law and of human rights, were permeated with concepts worked out by Christian reason and backed up by an unshakable religious feeling.

Jacques Maritain
Reflections on America[1]

---

[1](New York: Charles Scribner's Sons, 1958; rpt., Gordian Press, 1975) 182-83.

IV

Jacques Maritain had written in his great classic of 1936, *Humanisme Intégral,* of a "New Christendom," a new temporal civilization, a new political society on the historical horizon. He longed for a political order and culture that, as he wrote elsewhere, would be "religiously inspired and vitally Christian," while at the same time "secular in nature."[2] He envisioned a religiously plural society in which men and women of diverse faiths would cooperate freely to realize the common good of order and justice. Maritain created his vision of the ideal society using a philosopher's reason and sharpened intuition. He deduced the elements of justice from rational principles. He tried to picture Europe, and especially France, on the way to fulfilling this ideal. Yet, ironically, it was not until he came to America that he realized that a historical model existed for his ideal. He saw in America's Constitution, and in its historical evolution, a living experiment in precisely the kind of society he had envisioned.

[2]Ibid., 179.

Democratic pluralism and human rights are as much a product of history and human will as of reason and vision. For his part, Maritain first discerned the rational components of the just society and then sought to discover tendencies toward that ideal in the actual life of nations. Niebuhr, on the other hand, studied the historical patterns of political and religious development in order to extrapolate from them a logical and analytical theory of the just society. Both theologians thus forged political theologies that are at once rational and pragmatic. Both declared the goods of order and justice necessary in a free society; and both uncovered elements within Western cultural history through which these goods could be gradually realized.

Both Maritain and Niebuhr found in the American experiment an example-in-the-making of the just society they desired. Neither, however, idealized Western or American political development. They were often deeply critical of elements within that tradition. Each man lived through the tragic events of the twentieth century. Each observed at firsthand the life-or-death struggle of democracy with fascism and Communism, and with its own tendencies to disintegrate into factional strife. Yet they continued to hope that pluralist democracy, the vehicle of liberty and justice, would survive against the odds.

Order and Justice

The content of the political theologies of Maritain and Niebuhr can be understood through two basic categories: order and justice. A realistic Christian political theology, properly defined, accepts the fundamental axiom of political life that order is prerequisite to the realization of the forms of justice. Both theologians acknowledge that the inevitable and perpetual conflict of interests must be adjudicated by stable, lawful means. Politics is the art of settling conflicts without recourse to violence; in essence, it is war pursued by other means. When institutions of law and orderly procedures of governance are in place, then and only then does it become possible to pursue the expansion of justice in its various components: liberty, equality, fraternity. The full vision of a humane society in a fallen world includes both legitimate order and proximate justice.

In *The Structure of Nations and Empires,* Reinhold Niebuhr asserts the fundamental importance of order and analyzes the historical conflicts between the traditional establishment of order, always achieved with excessive force, and the progressive enlargement of justice through equalitarian reforms. Niebuhr finds that "all communities of mankind," whether tribe, nation, or empire, depended "upon some internal force of cohesion and . . . the unifying power of a central authority."[3] The sources of this cohesion and power are located in the community itself, which transmits to its political organ, the state, the essential "prestige" and "force" required for its functioning.

> "Power" and "authority" . . . describe the capacity of a government or state to gain obedience or compliance. The two sources of this power are "prestige" or "majesty"—which includes all the forces of tradition and history which induce obedience or compliance—and "force," the capacity to coerce.[4]

Niebuhr argues that a degree of order, ultimately guaranteed by the threat of coercion, is necessary to any political society. Force is a perennial feature of politics, according to Niebuhr's political theology, even though its exercise is "minimal in a well-established state." Force must be complemented with an acknowledged communal authority, a commonly held sense of an existing structure of law. "Coercion enforces obedience," Niebuhr observes, "until the authority of the government has been established, when it may win uncoerced consent by its prestige."[5] Similarly, Maritain defines the state as "an agency entitled to use power and coercion, and made up of experts or specialists in pub-

---

[3]Reinhold Niebuhr, *The Structure of Nations and Empires: A Study of the Recurring Patterns and Problems of the Political Order in Relation to the Unique Problems of the Nuclear Age* (New York: Charles Scribner's Sons, 1959; rpt., Fairfield NJ: Augustus M. Kelley, 1977) 33.

[4]Ibid., 8.

[5]Ibid.

lic order and welfare, an instrument in the service of man."[6] Public order is the beginning of the just society.

Niebuhr and Maritain affirm the heritage of centuries of Western political experience and Christian reflection upon politics, which combine to show that order is fundamental to justice. Niebuhr argues that history reveals a specific pattern in the establishment of order and justice. "Traditional communities, whether pagan or Christian, insisted on paying an excessive price in justice for the sake of order, because their order was never secure in the internal cohesions of the community." Such communities exist today in nations where authoritarian regimes exercise excessive force for the sake of maintaining order and stability. That order is itself a social good, but it is always less than just. By contrast, democratic pluralist nations, having already established a consensus regarding legitimate order, are involved in a constant process of establishing and refining justice. "Modern democratic communities . . . insist on justice, rather than order." This is the essence, according to Niebuhr, of all modern contributions to political life and theory. Reacting against traditional models, "modern democracies universally have thought the price in justice for the boon of order to be too high and have engaged in progressively equalitarian tendencies . . . [making] equality the regulative principle of justice."[7] Niebuhr points out that in the West religious reformers and rational idealists rebelled against the injustices of traditional communities. He links this fact to the economic developments in Western European life by which first the bourgeois and then the proletarian classes gained a voice in the formation of political policy. Such pluralism and differentiation of power was only possible after various forms of political, social, and economic cohesion existed, allowing for a more fluid system of political authority.

---

[6]Jacques Maritain, *Man and the State* (Chicago: University of Chicago Press, Phoenix Books, 1951) 13; Maritain's extended definition of the state is quoted below in the section "Maritain on Political Society."

[7]Niebuhr, *The Structure of Nations and Empires*, 4-5.

What, then, are the elements of the free society? *Order* is, of course, the primary value of society. It consists of a communal covenant to establish the rule of law among persons. It involves adherence to a constitution, which protects the basic interests of every group and individual in society. It implies a vital body politic, a competition of ideas in the public arena. Moreover, it presupposes a limited, instrumentalist, and accountable government or state, including a representative legislature, a responsible executive, and a free and fair judiciary.

Justice builds upon the foundation of legitimate order. It consists of liberty, equality, and fraternity gradually reconciled and actualized in the community. "Liberty" signifies the full range of human rights and civil liberties, and the successful limitation of the power of the state vis-à-vis the rights of citizens and groups. "Equality" stands for the complex web of law (primarily case law) that has rationally defined the requirements for the fair and uniform treatment of all citizens; that is, "equality before the law" and "equal opportunity." "Fraternity" encompasses the myriad relationships of individuals and institutions comprising the body politic, the welfare system that protects the weakest members of society, and the presence of a feeling of solidarity and cohesion that gives the community its particular identity and vitality. Liberty, equality, and fraternity are necessary to justice in a free society. The importance of fraternity to the other two is suggested by Maritain. "Justice is a primary condition for the existence of the body politic, but Friendship is its very life-giving form."[8]

This delineation of the major elements of order and justice in a fully developed political society is expressed by Maritain and Niebuhr in their own unique ways. Each has his own vocabulary and approach to the issue. I have already noted Maritain's tendency to rationalize and Niebuhr's frequent use of historical example. Beyond these simple differences, subtle, stylistic differences are present. Maritain constructs his analysis of pluralist democracy through a careful definition of community, society, the body politic, and the state; he then presents a defense

---

[8]Maritain, *Man and the State*, 10.

and detailed classification of the human, political, and economic rights of man. Niebuhr, by contrast, traces the development of ideas and practices that made possible the progressive realization of order, freedom, and equality within concrete historical experience. Yet the similarity of their visions is obvious from an examination of their concrete ideas.

Maritain on Political Society

For Maritain, the essence of pluralist democracy and human rights is found in the distinction between the idea of a limited state and the larger community that encompasses it. The opposite of the just society, and the modern archetype of tyranny, is totalitarianism—that form of government in which the power of the state has grown beyond its proper limits until it absorbs other elements of the community previously independent of its power. The key for Maritain is the idea that the body politic includes, in addition to the state, all of the various communities and institutions in which men and women choose to participate. The *entire* body politic is the arena for ascertaining the public will, but the state— only a part of the whole—is charged with carrying out that will. In politics, according to Maritain, there are things more fundamental than the state itself. The body politic transcends the state.

Maritain praised the United States for its "organic multiplicity" and resistance to excessive politicization and government control. "The American mind," Maritain observed, "still does not like the look of the very notion of *state*. It feels more comfortable with the notion of *community*."[9] Community or civil society includes not only the state but all of those institutions that mediate between the individual and the state. These "mediating structures" include families, churches, schools, voluntary associations, labor unions, business corporations, and so forth.[10] The balance of all these forces, along with a recognition of the legitimate rights of each, is the essence of democratic pluralism.

---

[9]Maritain, *Reflections on America*, 162-63.

[10]See the section "Mediating Structures and Economic Humanism."

So it is necessary, in analyzing Maritain's political theology, to focus on the idea of the state and its place within the larger context of civil society. The state is by no means the only expression of political society, although it is its principal institution. It is a *means*, not the *end* of politics. Beginning with the collective dimension of political life, embodied in state, society, and culture, it is possible to lay the foundations for the enumeration and realization of human rights and civic responsibility.

During the dark days of the Second World War, Maritain dreamed of a recovery of pluralist democracy, a renewal of political society inspired by a religious ethos. Maritain's hopes for the establishment of pluralist democracy were confirmed by the recovery of Europe after the war, the growth of justice and prosperity in the Free World generally, and the foundation of a world order in which the United Nations would play an influential role. Maritain's view of democracy was repeatedly clarified and refined in the succeeding years.

In 1944 Maritain condensed his vision of democratic pluralism in a little book entitled *Christianity and Democracy*. He noted a fundamental relationship between the gospel message of the Christian faith and the historical emergence of democracy. Since he was at that time unfamiliar with American democracy, he wrote with the European experience in mind. He contrasted the counterfeit notion that "Christianity is linked to democracy" (such that "Christian faith compels every believer to be a democrat") with the true claim that "democracy is linked to Christianity." "The democratic impulse," he wrote, "has arisen in human history as a temporal manifestation of the inspiration of the Gospel."[11] Thus Maritain located the roots of the democratic movement in Christianity, in the tradition of the church, and in the message of the Bible. Likewise, the movement for human rights is a manifestation of the spirit of the gospel, with its emphasis on the value of the individual and his conscience, its affirmation of the world, and its affirmation of all acts of love.

---

[11]Jacques Maritain, *Christianity and Democracy*, trans. Doris C. Anson (New York: Charles Scribner's Sons, 1944) 37.

Maritain developed his idea of democracy in light of his understanding of the relationship between religion and politics. His is a vision that emphasizes a community based on responsibility, a civic faith undergirded by a keen moral sense and a sincere spirituality. Maritain's political theology posits a belief in the necessity of a "religiously inspired and vitally Christian"[12] secular political society. Christian history at its best is a chronicle of the quest for peace and order in temporal life and the quest for conformity to the eternal reality of God's revelation concerning the sacred and the secular, religion and politics, church and state.

Christianity teaches that there is a vital distinction between the temporal political sphere of life and the eternal, spiritual sphere; but this in no way implies a final separation of religion from politics. Christian teaching affirms the truth of the statement by Mohandas K. Gandhi, which is inscribed over the entrance of the Gandhi Museum in Delhi, India: "I am told that religion and politics are different spheres of life. But I would say without a moment's hesitation and yet in all modesty that those who claim this do not know what religion is."[13] Similarly, Dietrich Bonhoeffer addressed the problem of the two realms by calling for an end to the dualism that separates civic life from the rigorous requirements of religious ethics. This led him to declare that "there are not two spheres, standing side by side, competing with each other and attacking each other's frontiers." Bonhoeffer discerned an ultimate unity of the two realms. He wrote, "The whole reality of the world is already drawn in into Christ and bound together in Him, and the movement of history consists solely in divergence and convergence in relation to this centre."[14]

Likewise, Maritain is opposed to separating the two realms; indeed, he seeks a society in which the political order approximates justice through an infusion of spiritual wisdom and righ-

---

[12]Maritain, *Reflections on America*, 179.

[13]See Erik H. Erikson, *Gandhi's Truth: On the Origins of Militant Nonviolence* (New York: W. W. Norton & Co., 1969) 22.

[14]Dietrich Bonhoeffer, *Ethics*, ed. Eberhard Bethge, trans. Neville Horton Smith (New York: Macmillan Co., 1955) 198.

teousness. For the individual, the life of faith cannot be separated from the parallel responsibility to cooperate with one's neighbor in the formation of justice based on order. For the collectivity, the inherited traditions of faith and the community provide the context of values and principles that legitimate or delegitimate the policies of the temporal authorities.

Far from a dualism of the spiritual and the political, there is a continuity, or analogy, between these two realms, as well as a perennial tension, or paradox. This means that the Christian teaching on politics will always include both the attitude of obedience and the attitude of dissent, an approach that is at once critical and responsible toward the established authorities. In this regard, on the one hand, the Christian must recognize the similitude of sacred and political authority in Paul's famous admonition: "Let every person be subject to the governing authorities. For there is no authority except from God and those that exist have been instituted by God. . . . [The ruler] is God's servant for your good" (Rom. 13:1, 4). On the other hand, Jesus' words regarding Caesar express a fundamental tension between faith and politics, echoing the harsh words of the prophets of ancient Israel like Amos who cried out, "Woe to those who are at ease in Zion" and "Let justice roll down like waters, and righteousness like an ever-flowing stream" (Amos 6:1; 5:24). Clearly, therefore, the doctrine of the two realms implies both an affinity and a tension between religion and politics.

In his book The Rights of Man and Natural Law, Maritain analyzes man's relation to the two realms. He points out that two statements by Thomas Aquinas illuminate the problem. First, "Every individual person bears the same relationship to the whole community as the part bears to the whole." Thus Maritain concludes that the "entire person" is engaged in politics, a truth that "anarchical individualism" denies. Second, Thomas argued, "Man is not ordered to political society by reason of all that is in him." In other words, says Maritain, "The entire human person is a part of political society . . . [and] also above political society."[15]

---

[15]Jacques Maritain, The Rights of Man and Natural Law, trans. Doris C. Anson (New York: Charles Scribner's Sons, 1943; rpt., New York: Gordian Press, 1971) 13-16.

Totalitarianism denies this transcendent, spiritual dimension of man.

The Christian doctrine of the two realms is a two-edged sword. It teaches that every person is a part of society. Since the good of the part is not greater than the good of the whole, individual interests are inferior to the interests of the common good. Each individual has an obligation to serve the common good. The ideology of "anarchical individualism" is false because it relieves the individual of his responsibility to the community. But the doctrine of the two realms also teaches that man is a spiritual being, a personality, and as such, must never be treated solely as a tool of the collective interest.

Totalitarianism of both the fascist and Communist types sacrifices the individual to a spurious myth of community. Maritain sees a prime example of the totalitarian subordination of individuals in Mussolini's slogan: "Everything in the State, nothing against the State, nothing outside of the State."[16] Similarly, Maritain rejects Rousseau's argument that the state is all, that the state is the only institution of political society, and that no *particular* society should be permitted in the state.[17] Maritain consistently opposes all forms of absolutism in politics. Statism denies the legitimacy of lesser loyalties, of partial interests, of institutions outside the apparatus of state control. This is why Maritain always criticized the Communist dogma of absolute party control. His political theory expresses, rather, the pluralist differentiation of forces in society and the existence of a vital and complex relation among those forces.

By comparison with statism, the Christian view of the state is centered not so much on structures as on persons. The end of politics is the common good of persons, but, to be genuine, this collective good must flow back to, and enrich, the individual.

---

[16]Benito Mussolini, *Scritti e Discorsi* (N.p., 1927); quoted in Jacques Maritain, *Integral Humanism: Temporal and Spiritual Problems of a New Christendom*, trans. Joseph W. Evans (New York: Charles Scribner's Sons, 1968; rpt., Notre Dame IN: University of Notre Dame Press, 1973) 283.

[17]Maritain, *Reflections on America*, 162.

Maritain echoes the definitions of political society elaborated by Aristotle and Thomas Aquinas; in Maritain's words, "Political society is a work of reason and virtue, and implies a will or consent to live together, which freely emanates from . . . the people."[18] These are the fundamental elements of political society: (1) reason, as opposed to passion; (2) virtue, which leads to justice; and (3) the genuine will to live together, which constitutes civic friendship.

Maritain constructs his political theory on the basis of rational definitions of the nation, political society, and the state. These definitions appear in the opening pages of the carefully reasoned summation of his political philosophy, *Man and the State*. This short book is one of the most lucid and penetrating analyses of Christian political theory every written. The outlines of the theory can be stated in a few short definitions.

> A preliminary distinction must be made . . . between *community* and *society*. . . . Both community and society are ethico-social and truly human, not mere biological realities. But a community is more of a work of nature and more nearly related to the biological; a society is more of a work of reason, and more nearly related to the intellectual and spiritual properties of man.

From this initial distinction there follow the definitions of the nation and the body politic (or political society). The national community is bound together by kinship and other forms of cohesion, and this precedes the formation of society as a work of reason with a framework of existing laws.

> The *Nation* is a community, not a society. . . . [It] originates . . . from the notion of *birth*, but the nation is not something biological, like the Race, it is something ethico-social. . . .
>
> The nation has . . . a soil, a land—this does not mean, as for the State, a territorial area of power and administration, but a cradle of life, work, pain, and dreams.

The nation is a community. The body politic is a society. Maritain

---

[18]Ibid., 168.

proceeds from the biological to the rational bases of human inter-action.

> In contradistinction to the *Nation*, both the *Body Politic* and
> the *State* pertain to the order of society. . . . We have to distin-
> guish clearly between the State and the Body Politic. These do not
> belong to two diverse categories, but they differ from each other
> as a part differs from the whole. The *Body Politic* or the *Political
> Society* is the whole. The *State* is a part—the topmost part—of this
> whole.

The body politic or political society is a work of deliberate reason.
The rational basis of this society includes but transcends the state.

> *Political society* . . . is the most perfect of temporal societies.
> . . . It is a work of reason, born out of the obscure efforts of reason
> disengaged from instinct, and implying essentially a rational or-
> der; but it is no more Pure Reason than man himself. . . . Justice
> is a primary condition for the existence of the body politic, but
> Friendship is its very life-giving form.[19]

On the subject of justice and friendship, Maritain had written
elsewhere, "While the structure of society depends primarily on
justice, the vital dynamism and the internal creative force of society depend on civic friendship."[20]

For Maritain, there must be a basic social cohesion, a stable order that, although backed up by the coercive power of the law, is
fundamentally a covenant of free men and women living according to an accepted standard of justice. The authority of the state
depends on such guarantees of order and justice.

> The State is only that part of the body politic especially con-
> cerned with the maintenance of law, the promotion of the com-
> mon welfare and public order, and the administration of public
> affairs. The State is a part which *specializes* in the interest of the
> *whole.* . . .
> The State is not the supreme incarnation of the Idea, as Hegel
> believed; the State is not a kind of collective superman; the State

---

[19]Maritain, *Man and the State*, 2, 4-6, 9, 10

[20]Maritain, *The Rights of Man and Natural Law*, 35.

is but an agency entitled to use power and coercion, and made up of experts or specialists in public order and welfare, an instrument in the service of man. Putting man at the service of that instrument is political perversion. The human person as an individual is for the body politic and the body politic is for the human person as a person. But man is by no means for the State. The State is for man.[21]

Maritain calls this an "instrumentalist" theory of the state, since in it "the State is inferior to the body politic as a whole, and is at the service of the body politic as a whole." The instrumentalist theory is the opposite of the despotic or absolutist theory of the state, in which the state is "superimposed on the body politic or made to absorb the body politic entirely."[22]

The instrumentalist theory of the state, and of political society, is one of the greatest treasures of Christian and humanist philosophy. It establishes the most radical and truly revolutionary idea in the whole realm of political life: the limits of the state. It is this idea that, over the course of centuries, has stood between the common man and the will-to-power of various religious, political, or economic elites seeking to impose their own will upon the community. It is an idea that challenges the existence of regimes based on brute force, whether that force is wielded by race, class, or party. It is also an idea that applies to democratic regimes in which the power of government has gradually become excessive.

Maritain constructs a theory of the just society by which both tyrannical and relatively free political systems can be judged. His warning about the excesses of the state is even more relevant today than when he wrote it.

Power tends to increase power, the power machine tends ceaselessly to extend itself; the supreme legal and administrative machine tends toward bureaucratic self-sufficiency; it would like to consider itself an end, not a means. . . . The State tends to ascribe to itself a peculiar common good—its own self-preservation and

---

[21]Maritain, *Man and the State*, 12-13.

[22]Ibid., 13-14.

growth—distinct from both the public order and welfare which are its immediate end, and from the common good which is its final end.[23]

The state, then, is dangerous when it becomes too powerful. If it remains an instrument in service to the common good, it fulfills its proper function. The legislative, executive, and judicial branches of the state exist as guardians of the public order and the welfare of the people. The people are prior to and superior to the structure of government that they establish. The people are prior to the state, just as the body politic is prior to the state. "The people," as Maritain puts it, "have a natural right . . . to self-government." It follows that political authority is the possession of the people, who assign this power to certain individuals and agencies without in any measure losing possession of it. For Maritain, "the most accurate expression concerning the democratic regime is not 'sovereignty of the people.' It is Lincoln's saying: 'government of the people, by the people, for the people.' "[24] This is Maritain's interpretation of Aristotle's ancient ideal: the will to live together emanating from the people.

What does this mean in concrete terms? Which type of state—monarchical, aristocratic, or democratic, using Aristotle's classification—is most compatible with the Christian idea? There is no "Christian" type of government or economy, but the different types can be more or less compatible with Christianity. That one form of government might be more fully conformed to the gospel is not to say that Christianity cannot and has not coexisted with every type of regime known to man. It has. Neither should Christianity sacralize a particular social order and attach its own fate to the fate of that order or culture. Nevertheless, the political humanism that is inspired by the gospel entails certain specific principles concerning the organization of the state.

Maritain recalls the three main types of polity identified in Aristotle's system of classification. Aristotle had surveyed every

[23]Ibid., 14.

[24]Ibid., 25.

existing constitution that he could find in the Mediterranean world of the fourth-century B.C. He collected 158 constitutions from the Greek states alone.[25] The monarchical regime, he concluded, seeks strength and unity. The aristocratic regime seeks the differentiation of values and attempts to nurture the noblest ones. The democratic regime seeks freedom. For Maritain, the best regime is a mixture of these three classic types "organically united." But, because of the importance of the human person and the progressive conquest of freedom that is taking place in history, the predominant mark of the body politic must be its democracy.

Democracy does not mean turning the masses into a god whose power is then consigned to the state. On the contrary, true democracy is "an advance toward justice and law and toward the liberation of the human being."[26] In a democracy, the control of the people over the state is permanently set forth in the constitution. Through the power of the vote the people have a "regular, statutory means of exercising their control." The elected representatives of the people must face a periodic evaluation at the ballot box, while they in turn exert continuous pressure on the behavior of the executive branch. Furthermore, through a free press, an open expression of public opinion, and the activities of pressure groups, other checks and balances to the power of the state are created.[27]

While these characteristics of democracy are known to all citizens of free societies, familiarity should not prevent recognition of their fundamental importance for maintaining a government of, by, and for the people. In order to appreciate the checks and balances of democratic pluralism, one need only compare the democratic experience with that of societies under absolutist regimes that substitute brute force for popular mandate and seek to control every dimension of human life for the convenience of the state and the increase of its power.

---

[25]W. D. Ross, *Aristotle: A Complete Exposition of His Works and Thought*, 5th rev. ed. (New York: World Publishing Co., Meridian Books, 1959) 229.

[26]Maritain, *The Rights of Man and Natural Law*, 51, 53.

[27]Maritain, *Man and the State*, 65.

At this point, the outlines of a Christian theory of the state, as Maritain understands it, should begin to take shape. The state is part of a broader society, the body politic, which is based on reason, virtue, and the will to live together. The state is the topmost part, and the servant, of the political society; this, in turn, is made up of the people, who assign to the state its authority. The state is devoted to the maintenance of law, the common welfare, the public order, and the administration of public affairs. Finally, the truly instrumental state is established and maintained through the power of the ballot—that is, by democratic consensus.

Mediating Structures and "Economic Humanism"

We discover the most fundamental insights of Christian political theory when we go beyond the immediate question of the mechanisms of government to explore more deeply the concept of the body politic. The body politic is the whole of which the state is only a part. The people make up the body politic and set for it— for themselves—the task of defending and serving the common good. Two further ingredients are required in the body politic: justice and friendship. Political society consists of those institutions in which persons freely choose to participate—including the family, the neighborhood, the ethnic group, the school, the communication medium, the labor union, the business enterprise, the voluntary association in its various forms, the political party, and the church. Some of these institutions, especially the family and church, exist as entities beyond the political society, but they are simultaneously a part of the *polis*. Thus political society covers a broad range of human activities and interactions; it reaches into, and is affected by, every aspect of culture. Maritain notes the importance of the various mediating institutions for a genuine body politic.

> All communities of the nation . . . [are] comprised in the superior unity of the body politic. But the body politic also contains in its superior unity the family units, whose essential rights and freedoms are anterior to itself, and a multiplicity of other particular societies which proceed from the free initiative of citizens and should be as autonomous as possible. Such is the element of pluralism inherent in every truly political society. Family, eco-

nomic, cultural, educational, religious life matter as much as does political life to the very existence and prosperity of the body politic.[28]

Political society, according to Maritain, is a specific instance of human activity within the general sphere of culture. Politics is a labor of reason and the virtues, an effort directed toward the goal of building a civilization, which must take place at the level of society. But, recalling Maritain's distinction between society and community, there is a deeper dimension of culture, "which relates to the rational development of the human being considered in all its generality." Culture includes all "intellectual, moral and spiritual development," as well as all political development. A politics of justice depends upon deep communal bonds of cohesion.

It is possible for a ruler to build up the material structure of a civilization while suppressing the cultural freedom of its people. The result, however, will be a brutish form of civilization—in other words, a pseudocivilization. Without the free play of a multitude of ideas and institutions, without cultural pluralism, it is impossible to build a truly just political order. Cultural pluralism is a key aspect of the Christian ideal for earthly life.

Maritain's philosophy of "integral humanism" places primary emphasis upon the creative activity of human persons coming together in a variety of institutions and social movements. These institutions are the social structures that mediate between the individual and the state. Every individual participates in a number of these institutions. They are the fundamental forms of expression for the individual, and they serve a crucial psychological function by facilitating the formation of personal identity.

Maritain recognized the importance of mediating institutions for the proper functioning of a pluralist body politic. He was especially impressed with the social differentiation that he found in the United States. "There is in this country a swarming multiplicity of particular communities," he wrote. In such a society, the idea of community is more at home than the idea of the state. Plu-

---

[28]Ibid., 11.

ralism is its watchword; Maritain called it "organic multiplicity." There is a "plurality of states" which have "grown into . . . a single Federal State." A vast number of voluntary associations—labor unions, vocational or professional associations, religious brotherhoods, interest groups with myriad causes—bring individuals together for the pursuit of common interests.[29]

While many theorists decry the prevalence of "interest-group politics," Maritain maintains that there is a place for the particular kind of competition that takes place in a pluralist democracy. People do have a right to organize to defend their own interests. Even "machine politics," though less noble than the rational ideals embodied in the Constitution, can be made to serve lofty principles. Each element of particular interest, when expressed within a truly pluralist society, advances the common interest, the common good, of all.

The significance of social institutions that remain independent of state control becomes especially clear in Maritain's analysis of industrial civilization. His reading of the history of democratic capitalism, or economic humanism, is central to his political vision, yet his social theory allows him to make an objective evaluation of the moral claims of capitalism and socialism. Maritain's mature view of the ideological conflict between capitalism and socialism hinges on his understanding of two mediating institutions that he considers indispensable in a modern, free society: the labor union and the business corporation. It is here that the significance of democratic capitalism in a pluralist society comes into bold relief.

"The old merciless struggles between management and labor," Maritain writes, "have given way to a new relationship." Both management and labor are discovering the virtue of "intelligent collective self-interest." "Corporations are becoming aware," he says, "of the primacy of welfare and the political common good." "Organized labor," also, has a "growing power" and a "growing sense, too, of the primacy of the general welfare and the political common good." "Free enterprise and private own-

---

[29]Maritain, *Reflections on America*, 162-63.

ership function now in a social context and a general mood entirely different from those of the nineteenth century."[30]

For most of his life, Jacques Maritain did not look kindly on corporations. He considered industrial civilization an "inhuman and materialist" form of idolatry.[31] Later his thinking underwent a change, however. By 1958 he had arrived at his final position that corporations played a vital role in pluralist democracy. Of course he still recognized that they were motivated by self-interest. "I do not assume that corporations have reached a stage where they would prefer the common good to their own particular good." Maritain, like Niebuhr, always emphasized the permanent tendency of each individual and social group to seek its own interests, even at the expense of the rights of others. "These big organisms . . . are still fondly thinking, to be sure, of the dividends of their stockholders—but not as the unique, even as the first thing; because they have understood that, in order simply to exist, and to keep producing, they must become more and more socially minded and concerned with the general welfare." They are becoming more responsible "not by reason of any Christian love, but rather of intelligent self-interest."[32]

Likewise, Maritain saw labor unions as institutions that were developing an increasing sense of social responsibility. He believed that the labor union was "becoming more deeply and organically basic in the whole economic process, . . . evolving from a merely antagonistic force . . . into a necessary and responsible counter-balancing power." Furthermore, "it confronts big corporations as an equal." The leaders of the labor union "try to get

---

[30]Ibid., 109, 197, 101. Maritain wrote much more about pluralism in the political and cultural spheres than about economic pluralism. Would that he had said more. Nevertheless, we can be grateful for his brief but suggestive chapter, "Too Much Modesty: The Need for an Explicit Philosophy," ibid. Although he was referring to the history of struggle between the American labor movement and business management and specifically to the hopeful signs he saw in the particular situation of the 1950s, his analysis is also applicable to pluralist societies in general.

[31]Ibid., 21.

[32]Ibid., 106-107.

the best possible conditions without putting the progress of pro-duction in jeopardy," for "the very power of labor needs great in-dustry as the very prosperity of great industry needs labor."[33]

Maritain began his career with a typical intellectual bias against capitalism, and later came to see the evolving institutions of democratic capitalism as vehicles of liberty. He saw the "in-human" industrial system gradually awakening to its obligations toward the general welfare. Maritain tells the story of a magazine editor who wrote an article entitled "Wanted: A New Name for Capitalism." The editor invited his readers to send in their sug-gestions. To his surprise, 15,000 replies came back. The sugges-tions included "industrial democracy," "economic democracy," "the new capitalism," "democratic capitalism," "distributiv-ism," "mutualism," "productivism," and "managementism." Maritain, too, felt the need for a new phrase to describe the inner transformation of the industrial regime. He suggested "economic humanism" as the term that best conformed to the broader per-sonalist and pluralist society that he envisioned. He advocated an economy in which every agent in the productive process, acting with intelligent self-interest, would receive his due proportion of the material reward. Further, there would be freedom to initiate a business for its possible rewards; there would be equality of op-portunity in a generally classless system, with a high degree of upward (and downward) social mobility; and there would be a bond of civic friendship to generate obligations to honesty and fairness in business dealings.[34]

The mediating institutions, including the labor union and the business enterprise, illustrate a basic principle of pluralist soci-ety: the necessity for numerous centers of power, each with its own ability to check and balance the others. The body politic in a plu-ralistic order is the aggregation of these power centers. The state is only one institution among many, although it is the topmost; and there is a diffusion of power even within the state. This plu-ralism of forces infuses the political order through democracy, the

---

[33]Ibid., 103-105, 109.

[34]Ibid., 112-13.

cultural order through reason, morality, and spirituality, and the economic order through intelligent self-interest.

Such a system of pluralism and balance of power is known by a number of names. Maritain spoke of a "political humanism" and an "economic humanism." Since his time, the term "democratic capitalism" has come to be used in a similar manner; it signifies not only a socially responsible system of economic production and distribution, but also a democratic political system and a pluralist culture as well.

Following the examples of Maritain and Niebuhr, the Roman Catholic philosopher Michael Novak has described democratic capitalism as a tripartite system of political, economic, and moral-cultural freedoms. Each of these social spheres, according to Novak, has a certain autonomy, yet each is a check and balance to the others. Like Maritain, Novak offers a critique of Soviet-style socialism as a system in which the political sphere has achieved hegemony over the economic and moral-cultural spheres. In such a system the power struggle is permanently unbalanced and therefore the polity inevitably becomes centralized and tyrannical. Democratic capitalism, on the other hand, stands for (1) political freedom achieved through representative democracy, (2) economic freedom based on incentives and market mechanisms, and (3) moral-cultural freedom attained through the open competition of ideas.[35] "Democratic capitalism," Novak argues, applies to all three spheres. He notes that it would be even more accurate to use the rather awkward phrase "democratic capitalist pluralism," which would signify the relative autonomy, and spirit of liberty, of each of the three spheres. Maritain likely would have found himself in substantial agreement with Novak.

Returning, for the moment, to the economic component of democratic pluralism, the important issue today is whether peoples and nations choose a system of socially responsible free enterprise based on incentives and market determinations of wages and prices—a social market economy—or a system of political

---

[35]See Michael Novak, The Spirit of Democratic Capitalism (New York: Simon & Schuster, 1982).

structures that centrally control the production and allocation of goods and services. This is the great debate between "markets" and "politics." The first is the way of individual freedom and the differentiation of power. The second is the way of a greater and more powerful state. Christian political theory, in its mainstream expressions, including the mature writings of Maritain and Niebuhr, has always defended the right to private property and the right to enjoy the fruits of one's labors.[36] Nevertheless, these rights are not unlimited. The rights of the person and of the common good must be balanced. Hence there have been evolving attempts to formulate the Christian doctrines of the just price and the just wage, the ban on usury, and the obligations to fair business dealings and charitable relief. The question that Christians face in the modern era is, "Which system, capitalism or socialism, best approximates the gospel ideal?" Should there be a relatively autonomous economic sphere with incentives and fair markets or a consolidation of political and economic decision-making in the hands of a dominant elite?

The record of Soviet-style socialism in the world is not impressive, measured by Maritain's criteria. Rigidly socialist policies have created stagnant economies and exacerbated poverty, although poverty existed long before either socialism or capitalism. Under many forms of socialism, the lack of economic freedom has been accompanied by restrictions on political, cultural, and religious freedoms. No nation subjected to a thorough socialist transformation at the hands of a party calling itself a socialist "vanguard" has ever achieved to date a restoration of multiparty democracy. The Soviet-style socialist state is an intrusive and pervasive state. It is an indignity for a person to be subjected to comprehensive state control of his speech, his movements, his purchases and contracts, his association with others, his political beliefs, and even his religious beliefs and worship.

The Christian view rejects statist and totalitarian systems, the forced unification of politics, economics, and culture. Instead,

---

[36]See the discussion of Maritain's view of private-property rights in the section "Maritain's Concept of Human Rights."

Christianity proclaims itself compatible with a pluralist order that delineates the distinct and complementary powers of each sphere. This is the social philosophy that Jacques Maritain professed and, as we shall see, it held true also for Reinhold Niebuhr. Maritain argued that the roots of such a pluralist society are found in the Judeo-Christian tradition. Maritain's religious insights into the problems of the political order are embodied in his definitions of the body politic, the state, mediating institutions, and culture. A viable political ethic must recognize, with Maritain, that society is a work of "reason and the virtues. . . . [It is a] work of the spirit and liberty."[37]

Maritain's Concept of Human Rights

Maritain's idea of a political society, with a diversity of institutions and power centers, is directly related to his philosophy of personalism, with its emphasis on the rights of the human person. Human rights signifies, for Maritain, the full range of personal, political, and economic rights of man. Maritain based his extensive analysis of human rights on the vision of a vital body politic in which men and women freely participate, and on the idea of a limited and instrumentalist state.

"Human rights" is a watchword of our times. The phrase evokes a shining image of the global community—all four and one-half billion of the earth's inhabitants—sharing together in a universal respect for each other's dignity and dreams. Reality, of course, has a much harder lesson to teach. Most nations today, as in the past, remain unfree. The phrase "human rights" suggests a political philosophy dedicated to the idea that the state must serve man—not the reverse—and that state power must be limited. The idea of a global family is today a powerful symbol that calls upon all persons to work to build truly just political societies everywhere in the world. The largeness of this vision need not, however, cause nations to drift into utopianism and rob the human

---

[37]Maritain, The Social and Political Philosophy of Jacques Maritain: Selected Readings, ed. Joseph W. Evans and Leo R. Ward (New York: Charles Scribner's Sons, 1955; rpt., Notre Dame IN: University of Notre Dame Press, 1976) 217.

rights movement of its realism, its practicality—for practicality is the very key to agreement on questions of human rights. Jacques Maritain was one of the preeminent theorists of human rights in the twentieth century, an influential voice when the United Nations was established, and one of the authors of its Universal Declaration of the Rights of Man.

Maritain tells the following story about the vast differences that sometimes separate persons from different nations. He refers specifically to those who took part in the formulation of the United Nations' Universal Declaration of the Rights of Man, which was unanimously adopted in 1948. The French delegation was composed of an assortment of individuals, some with radically opposed ideologies. Yet they had been able to agree on a list of rights they could all support. One observer was astonished. He asked how it was possible for such a diverse group to agree on anything. The answer came back, "Yes, we agree on these rights, providing we are not asked why." Their agreement was purely practical; with regard to theories, they agreed to disagree. Their situation was a microcosm of the United Nations as a whole.

Maritain sought an answer to this question of how a global community could agree on a set of practical principles that would increase the chances for justice, peace, and development in the world. He was addressing the second International Conference of UNESCO (The United Nations Educational, Scientific and Cultural Organization), meeting in Mexico City in November of 1947.

> How is an agreement conceivable among men . . . who come from the four corners of the earth and who belong not only to different cultures and civilizations, but to different spiritual families and antagonistic schools of thought? . . . Agreement . . . [can be achieved] not on the affirmation of the same conception of the world, man, and knowledge, but on the affirmation of the same set of convictions concerning actions.

It was, he said, "very little" to go on, but "enough to undertake a great work."[38] In his book *Man and the State*, Maritain attempts

---

[38]Maritain, *Man and the State*, 77-78.

to delineate a possible basis for agreement among persons from all regions of the earth, a common ground for nations with divergent interests. They should have, he says, a similar reverence (although for quite diverse reasons) for "truth and intelligence, human dignity, freedom, brotherly love, and the absolute value of moral good."[39] The basis of world order, then, is practical agreement and a similar reverence for truth and morality, even if those terms must remain somewhat ill defined.

This is a difficult issue. On the one hand, Maritain asserts the truth of the Thomistic view of man and natural law: the concept of human rights is grounded in Absolute Truth. Yet he argues for a purely practical agreement among nations, recognizing their fundamental divergence on matters of ultimate concern. Perhaps Maritain is not so much inconsistent on this point as he is simply realistic about what his audience will accept. He believes in Truth, but he will settle for even an uneasy ideological truce.

Maritain's argument is not unlike the one made by Walter Lippmann, the widely read political commentator, during the Second World War. Lippmann wondered whether true peace would come after the Allied victory; he hoped it would involve the formation of an alliance of "Britain, Russia, America, and, if possible, China." Though his vision proved overly optimistic, his argument still carries a germ of truth.

> Not all peoples everywhere and always have had the same conception of their essential liberties. But whatever they regard as their essential liberties, be they the liberties of the Christian West or of the Moslem world, or of the Hindus, or of the Chinese, it is these liberties which must be respected under the law if the power behind the law is to endure.

For Lippmann, as for Maritain, the common ground of respect for human rights is indeed closely related to the question of world peace.

> The East and the West have been formed in widely different cultural traditions. But what can prevail everywhere . . . is the uni-

---

[39]Ibid., 111.

versal law that force must not be arbitrary, but must be exercised in accordance with laws that are open to discussion and are subject to orderly revision. . . .

The great powers must become the organizers of an order in which the other peoples find that their liberties are recognized by laws that the great powers respect and that all peoples are compelled to observe.

If this is done, the new order will rest not on sentiment but on enlightened interest. Then only will it be strong enough to have authority. Then only will it be liberal enough to have its authority persist.[40]

Lippmann and Maritain both believed that the basis of cooperation between diverse peoples—and, hence, the basis of world order—must be a will to live together in practical agreement concerning common tasks, and in theoretical disagreement over the rationale for these same tasks. Nevertheless, there must be a similar reverence for a higher, or "universal" law, for truth, and for moral restraints—especially moral restraints upon the use of force. Furthermore, the building of such a world order requires a systematic defense of those "essential liberties" that today are called human rights.

In Maritain's opinion, human rights theory necessarily implies a view of man that encompasses both the social and individual aspects of human nature, and also recognizes that man has a spiritual destiny that transcends the political sphere. Maritain argues that a human being is simultaneously an individual and a person. By this he means that humans are both material and spiritual beings. "Our whole being is an individual by reason of that in us which derives from matter, and a person by reason of that in us which derives from spirit."[41] It is crucial for human rights theory that man's spiritual destiny be acknowledged. In this way the

---

[40]Walter Lippmann, U. S. Foreign Policy: Shield of the Republic (Boston: Little, Brown & Co., Atlantic Monthly Press, 1943) 171, 174-75.

[41]Jacques Maritain, The Person and the Common Good, trans. John J. Fitzgerald (New York: Charles Scribner's Sons, 1947; rpt., Notre Dame IN: University of Notre Dame Press, 1966) 43.

essential rights of the person are understood to lie outside the control of earthly, and fallen, institutions.

Jesus said to his disciples, "You are not of the world, but I chose you out of the world" (John 15:19). The Bible acknowledges our material, fleshly, and sinful nature, but calls us to a destiny that is spiritual and God-centered. Maritain's theory reflects this biblical doctrine of man.

Furthermore, the Bible emphasizes human dignity as well as human sinfulness. This complex view of human nature is essential to a realistic theory of human rights. "God created man in his own image . . . male and female he created them" (Gen. 1:27). God gave man authority over all the earth, making man his representative, his viceroy. Thus man had the authority to give names to all the animals, and God commanded him to "be fruitful and multiply, and fill the earth and subdue it" (Gen. 1:28). Yet human dignity is not total; humankind is permanently burdened with a freedom to choose good or evil. The Psalmist prays, "What is man that thou art mindful of him?" (Ps. 8:24). And Paul writes, "All have sinned and fall short of the glory of God" (Rom. 3:23).

Among all the world's religions, Judaism, Christianity, and Islam have most consistently emphasized the dignity and sinfulness, the rights and responsibilities, of the individual person. Under the influence of Christian teaching, modern Western thought generated a world view with humanity at the center. Because we have dignity, our rights and destiny must be respected. Because we are prone to sin, pride, and selfishness, we also must be restrained; we must be held accountable; and we must finally face a divine judgment concerning our individual actions. As Maritain observed, the historical development of the idea of human rights is bound up with the inspiration of the gospel at work in the world.

> The consciousness of the dignity of the person and of the rights of the person remained implicit in pagan antiquity—over which the law of slavery cast its shadow. It was the message of the Gospel which suddenly awakened this consciousness. . . . Under the

evangelical impulse, this same awakening was little by little
spread forth . . . over the realm of man's life here on earth.[42]

Maritain speaks of the gospel as a leaven at work in the world
that pushed man on toward democratic self-government and respect for human rights. Maritain correctly asserts that the concepts of man and of human rights in the American Declaration of
Independence and Constitution are directly rooted in an intellectual tradition that is also a theological tradition. Perhaps the most
influential forerunner of the theorists of the American Revolution
was John Locke, who was indirectly influenced by the natural
rights theory of Thomas Aquinas.[43]

Whenever Maritain gives his definition and analysis of human rights, he always begins in one way: by linking human rights
theory and natural law theory. "The philosophical foundation of
human rights," says Maritain, "is Natural Law."[44] Where the idea
of a natural law is alive, there also one finds the idea of human
rights; where it is corrupted, so too is human rights theory. For
Maritain, the doctrine of natural law is a complex and vital one:
it presupposes that there is such a thing as human nature—a belief that does not go unchallenged today—and that man has the
intelligence and will to choose the ends and goals he will pursue.
Of course, every person has certain ends that are shared with every
other person, such as health, happiness, and psychological
wholeness. Each of us may pursue these "natural" ends of human

[42]Maritain, The Rights of Man and Natural Law, 68.

[43]"Locke . . . was familiar with the great medieval tradition of politics to which
modern liberty owes so much: the tradition that government emanates from the
community, is subordinate to law, and must seek the popular welfare. He had
learned this doctrine from his reading of Richard Hooker" (Thomas P. Peardon,
introduction to The Second Treatise of Government, by John Locke, ed. Thomas
P. Peardon [Indianapolis: Bobbs-Merrill, Library of Liberal Arts, 1952] xi). However, see the comments on Locke's "tendentious reading of Hooker" in order to
justify the doctrine of the social contract in Alexander Passerin d'Entreves, The
Medieval Contribution to Political Thought: Thomas Aquinas, Marsilius of
Padua, Richard Hooker (Oxford: Oxford University Press, 1939; rpt., New York:
Humanities Press, 1959) 125-29.

[44]Maritain, Man and the State, 80.

existence, or we may deny them and choose to act self-destructively. God gives everyone freedom to choose. Therefore, it is possible to speak consistently of natural law *and* the freedom of will and conscience.

While Protestants may be unfamiliar with the terminology of natural law theory and may have only a minimal knowledge of Thomas Aquinas—the single most renowned Christian advocate of natural law theory—the doctrine nevertheless has a vital place in Christian theology.[45] The Bible teaches that God's ways are not man's ways, and that there is a divine standard to which the laws of society and the behavior of human persons do not always conform. The idea of a higher law is irrefutably a biblical concept. Roman Catholics and Protestants usually differ over whether, and to what degree, something in human *nature* is directed toward God's law. That something is indeed in conflict with man's propensity to selfishness and sin. Yet the logic of life, and of all human actions that affirm life, leads to the inevitable conclusion that there is, in some sense, a "natural law" in humankind. Roman Catholics and Protestants ought to be able to agree on this modest point.

Maritain argues that human rights and natural law cannot be separated. The reason is that "the same natural law which lays down our most fundamental duties . . . is the very law which assigns to us our fundamental rights." We possess rights vis-à-vis other men because we are enmeshed in (1) the universal order, (2) the laws and regulations of the cosmos, (3) the laws and regulations of the immense family of created natures, and (4) the order of creative wisdom. According to Maritain, "every right possessed by man" is possessed by virtue of God's right "to see the order of His wisdom in beings respected . . . and loved by every intelligence."[46] The first principle, which determines both the rights and the duties of man, is this: "Do good and avoid evil." God's order of wisdom has this as its first principle: "Seek righ-

---

[45]See ch. 2, under "Maritain's Dynamic View of Natural Law," and ch. 3, under "Maritain and Niebuhr on Aquinas's Natural Law."

[46]Maritain, *Man and the State*, 95-96.

teousness, avoid sin." Jesus said, "Blessed are those who hunger and thirst for righteousness, for they shall be satisfied" (Matt. 5:6).

The idea of man's spiritual destiny as person, and the idea of his calling to righteousness are aspects of a higher law infused in the relative, written laws of man. Thus the laws of a just society must respect "man's right to existence, to personal freedom, and to the perfection of the moral life." These most fundamental rights of man are inalienable because "they are grounded on the very nature of man, which . . . no man can lose."[47]

There is a false view of human rights that arises, according to Maritain, from a false view of human nature. The philosophers of the eighteenth century, especially Rousseau, had falsely held that "man is not subject to any law except that of his will and his liberty, and . . . he should 'obey only himself.' "[48] This Enlightenment view of man as maker of his own law spoke of "Nature with a capital N and Reason with a capital R," as if the human act was conformed to a preexisting pattern of perfect geometric regularity. Pascal had even believed that the laws of social and political justice must be like Euclid's propositions. Not only was the idea of nature made mechanistic, but so was the idea of natural law. The "fatal mistake" was to conceive natural law "as a *written* code, applicable to all, of which any just law should be a transcription, and which would determine *a priori* . . . the norms of human behavior."[49] The true theory of natural law, says Maritain, is God-centered not man-centered, and it presupposes not a predetermined, fixed view of man and moral action but a dynamic, open one. Man's moral life is a conquest of freedom. Much of the resistance to natural law theory today is, in fact, a rejection of this false and deterministic notion of "natural law."

Thus human rights theory depends upon a true view of human nature in all its complexity. Man is a creature, with creaturely limitations. Yet man is also a spiritual being, a person, whole, an end in himself, and not merely a means. He has a com-

---

[47]Ibid., 100-101.

[48]Maritain, *The Rights of Man and Natural Law*, 66-67.

[49]Maritain, *Man and the State*, 81-83.

plex set of rights, and corresponding duties, because of the complexity of his personhood.

What are these specific rights of man? Maritain divides them into three categories: the rights of the person as such, the rights of the civic person (or political rights), and the rights of the working person (or economic rights). A complete set of singular and concrete rights follows from the theoretical foundation that Maritain sets forth. However, seldom in history have these rights been acknowledged, and today only a few nations enjoy the full range of liberty that is man's inalienable right.

Probably no thinker before or since Maritain has enunciated so thorough a listing of specific human rights. He includes fundamental notions of human dignity and freedom in every aspect of human life: (1) "the right to existence," (2) "the right to personal liberty"; in other words, the right "to conduct one's own life as master of oneself and of one's acts, responsible for them before God and the law of the community," and (3) "the right to pursue perfection of moral and rational human life." Furthermore, man has a "right to pursue eternal life in the way conscience has seen as the way marked out by God." The church and other religious groups have rights to the "free exercise of their spiritual activity." Persons have a "right to follow a religious vocation." Other rights that belong to the person as such include "the right to marry according to one's choice and to establish a family," "the right to legal protection of the family," "the right to bodily integrity," which means, in general, "the right of each human being to be treated as a person, not as a thing," and "the right to the private ownership of material goods."[50]

At this point it may be illustrative to focus for a moment on the right to private property. Maritain argues that the right to private property belongs to man not only as economic or working person but also to the "human person as an extension of the person himself," because material goods are used for the "protection of his existence and freedom." Possessions are an extension of ourselves, and a defense against misfortune. On the other hand, how-

---

[50]Maritain, *The Social and Political Philosophy of Jacques Maritain*, 41-44.

ever, "the use of private property must always be such as to serve the common good in one way or another and to be advantageous to all."[51] It is important to preserve the right to private property, the right of the individual and the family to enjoy the fruits of their labors.

Christianity's emphasis on the individual has been a vital source of the modern concepts of man, work, and private property. The Christian faith has consistently affirmed the right to possess property, including productive property. In the days of the early church in Jerusalem, as described in the Book of Acts, the communal sharing of material goods was a voluntary act of brotherly love that was prompted by hardship. The early Christians held all the wealth in common and distributed it according to need. This act was in response to persecution and was not based on a denial of the right to private property. By way of contrast, there was at that time another religious sect, the Essenes, who practiced the involuntary and coerced surrender of private property rights, and transferred this right to the collectivity. This was clearly not the case with the early church. Christian doctrine has never seen the individual as a mere part of the whole, a cog in the social machine.

Next, there are the political rights of man, or "the rights of the civic person." Every adult citizen has a right to participate actively in political life and a right to equal suffrage, since voting is a primary form of participation. The people have a right "to decide for themselves their form of government" and "to establish the constitution of the body politic." Furthermore, there is "the right of association . . . and in particular the right to form political parties or political schools." All persons have a right to "freedom of expression," including the "right to free investigation and discussion" of every issue. Every citizen has a right to equality before the law, to equal protection of all the rights under discussion here, and especially the guarantee of an independent judiciary power. Finally, there must be "equal opportunity of admission to public employment"—the state cannot practice discrimination in

---

[51]Ibid., 39n.

public hiring—and there must be free access to the various professions.[52]

The last category of rights is economic, the rights of the working person. Each person has the right to choose his work, his vocation. From this there follows the right freely to form professional groups and trade unions; and such organizations have a right to freedom and autonomy. Workers have "a right to a just wage" (a living wage for themselves and their families), and where possible, "the right of joint ownership and joint management of the enterprise." Finally, whether or not someone is an economically productive member of society, he or she has a "right to assistance from the community in case of want, unemployment, sickness, or old age." Each person has a stake in, and a claim to, the material and spiritual goods of civilization.[53]

This list of the rights of man constitutes a map of the just political society. No individual or group, no state, can legitimately deny these rights to anyone, although some of these rights may be temporarily suspended in times of emergency. These rights belong to each individual because he is a person, because of his human nature as such, and because, in the Christian view, there is a natural law and a divine law that determine the rights and duties of man.

By the same token, every person has a civic responsibility to participate in collective life. Christian teaching encourages participation in the body politic and in activities that improve and perfect society. The basis for cooperation, especially among persons with differing religious outlooks, is a common "civic faith." This civic faith consists of a will to live together and to cooperate in practical ways that preserve human dignity, freedom, and equality.

The society of human rights and civic responsibility that Maritain described is an ideal. No existing society embodies this ideal. Nonetheless, every society has an obligation to move toward greater realization of this free society. In contemporary American

---

[52]Ibid., 44, 42.

[53]Ibid., 44.

society many of these rights and duties are generally observed; others are still less than fully realized. For example, American society continues to struggle with the issues of just wages, joint ownership, and joint management for workers. And the American people as a whole have not sufficiently fulfilled their duties of political participation, their civic responsibilities. Americans are shocked year after year by the low voter turnout in elections at various levels of government. Much work remains to be accomplished in building a just political society in the United States, just as much work remains in the other democratic societies.

The global status of human rights is even more discouraging. There are many nations in which even the most fundamental human rights are systematically denied. There are such regimes on both the ideological left and right. Past and present history is filled with examples of authoritarian and totalitarian regimes. As the technical tools of modern civilization have advanced, so also has the power of states to control and to coerce individuals and groups. Statism is as prevalent today as in the past, and it is increasingly pervasive.

The realities of the political world we inhabit provide grim testimony to the need for a vision of human rights and civic responsibility. Maritain's contribution to this task was to elaborate a rational structure of rights and responsibilities. This structure, if put into practice, would lead to a temporal realization of legitimate order and proximate justice. It would be an order and a justice that conform to the goals of Christian political theology as it is properly understood.

Niebuhr on Political Authority

The contemporary political world is in turbulence. While unprecedented prosperity and freedom have existed in a number of nations, much of the twentieth century has been as bloody, coercive, and brutish as earlier eras. The fruits of pluralist democracy are enjoyed in only a small percentage of the world's nations. Such freedom is often imperiled from within and from without. Most nations struggle to achieve even a minimum of order and stability, while the achievement of a significant measure of justice remains only a dream for the future.

Reinhold Niebuhr understood the reality of our turbulent modern world. He observed the tortuous historical process by which nations have tried successfully or unsuccessfully to establish a legitimate political order and to achieve proximate justice. Niebuhr analyzed the historical trends, the world-changing ideas, and the watershed events by which democratic pluralism and human rights came into being or failed to materialize. An analysis of Niebuhr's contribution to a political theology of democratic pluralism and human rights must focus on his understanding of the historical human struggle for order and justice. It was in history, in the concrete efforts of man to achieve a tolerable communal existence, that Niebuhr discerned the structures of power, nationhood, and empire. He discovered how often the ruling members of various societies have exerted their will by the force of sheer coercion, equating the success of nation and empire with the divine will. But he also found that, at certain times, democratic governments were formed that could lay fair claim to legitimacy. Modern history had disclosed, along with its horrors, some instances of freedom, some realizations of justice in an open society. It is this historical experience, the actual embodiment of democratic pluralism, which serves as Niebuhr's model for healing the turbulent world of today. And it is this process that Niebuhr can teach us.

In one of his last major books, *The Structure of Nations and Empires*, Niebuhr analyzes the "recurring patterns and problems of the political order"[54] from a truly world-historical perspective. He is particularly concerned to show how the relation of religion and politics had given a unique character to each of the major civilizations and empires from the days of ancient Egypt and Babylon to the present. Kings and magnates from time immemorial have claimed to be acting on behalf of a "great god," as agents of the gods of their own people and of the gods of their conquered subjects.[55] Niebuhr cites many examples of the religious and ideological legitimations employed by various rulers. He decries the

---

[54]This phrase appears in the subtitle of the book.

[55]Niebuhr, *The Structure of Nations and Empires*, 37.

uncritical manner in which religion is used to justify the crimes committed by tyrants. But he warns that their rhetoric is not to be understood as pure fraud. It is, rather, a necessary tool for earning the prestige required for the existence and maintenance of authority.

Every human community—tribe, city-state, nation, and empire—depends, according to Niebuhr, upon forces of internal cohesion expressed in some agency of central authority. Thus the element of coercive force itself, and the cultural infrastructure of legitimacy, are combined in every political entity. Ultimately, the sources of all authority are deeply rooted in the community itself. There are two main sources of authority for every regime: prestige and force. For Niebuhr, "authority" and "power" denote the ability of the state to gain compliance with its commands. The two sources of authority are " 'prestige' or 'majesty'—which includes all the forces of tradition and history which induce obedience or compliance—and 'force,' the capacity to coerce."[56]

At the beginning of a revolution, force may be the sole source of authority that a government possesses. But in order to survive, that government must eventually win the uncoerced consent of the governed by reason of its prestige, majesty, and legitimacy. Legitimacy comes when order is established and partial justice is realized, when the people freely offer their obedience and feel themselves to be represented by their rulers. In such a state, one that is most fully realized in a pluralist democracy, coercion is kept to a minimum. Where there is true authority, it has built a superstructure of prestige and legitimacy on a substructure of force.

Niebuhr wisely warned that coercion would never cease to exist in the political life of sinful humanity. But he argued that recognizing the necessity of force need not undercut the desire to minimize it. His accomplishment was to identify the deeper dimensions of political legitimacy while remaining realistic about the perennial factor of coercion in maintaining that legitimacy.

Niebuhr's political theology can be understood through his concepts of order and justice. These two boons of social existence

---

[56]Ibid., 8.

must arise from the two sources of authority already defined, namely, force and prestige. Force, and the coercive threat of force, establish the social good of order. Prestige comes as a result of the progressive realization of justice.

The prestige or legitimacy of a government is intimately bound up with the culture and collective memory of a people. Once chaos has been eliminated and stability is assured, a civilization seeks to ensconce itself in a system of laws, a predictable code of conduct and judgment. Though often frustrated, man naturally seeks a government that represents and protects him and mirrors his identity. The people of a civilization may call their political society a historical experiment, a social contract, a propositional endeavor. To build a civilization is to believe in a cause. A political society is a concrete, embodied reality.

Maritain located the definition of democratic pluralist civilization in Lincoln's phrase "government of the people, by the people, and for the people."[57] John Courtney Murray echoed this expression of the nature of legitimate authority in his discussion of the "American Proposition."

> To the early Americans government was not a phenomenon of force, as the later legal positivists would have it. Nor was it a "historical category," as Marx and his followers were to assert. Government did not mean simply the power to coerce, though this power was taken as integral to government. Government, properly speaking, was the right to command. It was authority. And its authority derived from law. By the same token its authority was limited by law. . . .
>
> Constitutionalism, the rule of law, the notion of sovereignty as purely political and therefore limited by law, the concept of government as an empire of laws and not of men—these were ancient ideas. . . . By the constitution the people define the areas where authority is legitimate and the areas where liberty is lawful. The constitution is therefore at once a charter of freedom and a plan for political order.[58]

---

[57]Maritain, *Man and the State*, 25.

[58]John Courtney Murray, *We Hold These Truths: Catholic Reflections on the American Proposition* (New York: Sheed & Ward, 1960; rpt., Garden City, NY: Doubleday & Co., Image Books, 1964) 43-44.

Similarly, Niebuhr argues that political authority goes beyond the simple power of coercion to include the element of prestige brought about by a common loyalty to the rule of law. This authority exists not simply because of the *rational* consent of the people, a commonplace illusion, but by an organic, cultural, and religious affinity that provides the vital social energy of constitutionalism. The rootedness of democratic pluralism is made clear in Niebuhr's use of history as the primary datum of political theology.

Niebuhr argues that the emergence of order and justice in Western history, both as concepts and as realities, came about by a particular pattern of progression: first, order, then the gradual realization of justice. Niebuhr observes that traditional political structures depended more on force and were able to provide the primary good of order, but could provide only a minimum of social justice. This was because the internal cohesion of traditional societies was too inadequately developed to provide the security necessary for the pursuit of justice. "Traditional communities," according to Niebuhr, "depended upon an undue emphasis upon the authority of the ruler and upon the value of the boon of order which his authority maintained."[59] Thus ancient rulers held absolute power and defended their exclusive monopoly of force in order to pursue order as their primary objective. The degree of justice that was realized depended on the good will of benevolent dictators and was not attained through the exertions of one power center against others.

It was not until the modern period that political life in the West came to be generally characterized by a plurality of social groupings, each demanding a minimum of justice and fair treatment from other, opposing groupings. The modern era saw the emergence of democratic, pluralist civilizations. According to Niebuhr, modern democratic communities have demanded a new kind of order that operates in conjunction with effective mechanisms for assuring justice, and these communities "have made

---

[59]Niebuhr, *The Structure of Nations and Empires*, 4.

equality the regulative principle of justice."[60] This new kind of order replaces absolutism with constitutionalism, and it shifts the criterion of effective government from stability to justice. This justice is defined by the equality of all citizens in a democratic state, balanced against the liberty of each individual—the ability of each individual to secure the rights due him from others and from the state.

Niebuhr described this process of establishing proximate justice through a balance of liberty and equality in a 1957 essay for the *Yale Review,* which appeared later in his book *Pious and Secular America.* In "Liberty and Equality," Niebuhr argued that neither principle of justice can be totally or uncritically exalted without destroying the community. Equality, the favorite criterion of justice for liberalism, is an effective tool for criticizing the social hierarchy. It is a valid tool because, while every political community necessarily relies upon a certain differentiation and gradation of its citizens, such hierarchies inevitably become disproportionate. Excessive privileges are dispensed to the ruling groups and the ruled masses suffer inequality. Under democratic pluralism, governments are forced constantly to answer the demand for equality as a regulative principle of justice. According to Niebuhr, this process has yielded an "equilibrium of organized power" that has "refuted the catastrophic predictions of Marxism and rendered the Western world safe against revolutionary resentment."[61] Nevertheless, the claim of equality does not finally overcome the need for social hierarchy.

Liberty, which is the preferred criterion of justice for conservatism, offers a perennial criticism of the community's "chief organ of unity and will," that is, "the police power of the state."[62] The unity of traditional communities demanded that government permit as little dissent as possible, and that it enforce conformity and devotion to the collectivity. This pattern was challenged in

---

[60]Ibid., 5.

[61]Reinhold Niebuhr, *Pious and Secular America* (New York: Charles Scribner's Sons, 1958; rpt., Fairfield NJ: Augustus M. Kelley, 1977) 65.

[62]Ibid., 62.

the modern era by the democratic-pluralist principle of liberty, especially the liberty of the individual. The collectivity no longer could claim the right to disregard the individual's "hopes, fears, and ambitions which are in conflict with, or irrelevant to, the communal end."[63] Liberty, like equality, became a regulative principle of justice. Ultimately, however, the claim of liberty cannot overrule the need for a political community to demand some measure of unity from its component groups and members. "Liberty is just as unrealizable in the absolute sense and just as relevant as the principle of equality."[64]

Niebuhr noted the significance of the idea of equality as a principle of justice in ancient Greek Stoicism. But Stoic equalitarianism failed to dislodge the class structure of traditional communities because it relegated equality to a mythical "golden age." It was not until the dawn of the modern age that a realistic concept of equality emerged and was joined with liberty in the formulation of the idea of justice.

Niebuhr argues that the Christian faith was instrumental in the emergence of the ideas of equality and the freedom of the individual. He cites Christianity's emphasis on "the uniqueness of the individual" and its "belief that the individual had a source of authority and an ultimate fulfillment transcending the community."[65] This gospel leaven at work in history revealed the truth of the principle of liberty. It was John Milton, says Niebuhr, who finally captured this ideal when he interpreted the scriptural command "Give unto Caesar the things that are Caesar's, and to God the things that are God's" to mean "My conscience I have from God and I can therefore not give it to Caesar."[66] Niebuhr cites this key statement by Milton in the introductory outline to *Man's Nature and His Communities*,[67] which he calls the "summary of my life-

---

[63]Ibid., 66.

[64]Ibid., 67.

[65]Ibid., 68.

[66]Ibid., 69.

[67]Niebuhr, *Man's Nature and His Communities: Essays on the Dynamics and Enigmas of Man's Personal and Social Existence* (New York: Charles Scribner's Sons, 1965) 26, 29.

work." In this context it clearly serves as a central theme in Niebuhr's understanding of the doctrine of the two realms.

Behind the question of the intellectual origins of the ideas of liberty and equality, according to Niebuhr, are some crucial modern developments in the class structure of Western societies. The commercial middle class awoke to its own power and broke the pattern by which the traditional community exerted an overweening demand for unity. Mobile forms of property and the mechanisms of incentives and rewards for individual initiative were the key to the phenomenal economic growth of the modern period and the guarantee of liberties not previously realized in history. On the heels of the bourgeois revolution came the proletarian demands for their own voice in the democratic control of political power. While the bourgeoisie had emphasized liberty, the working classes advocated more equalitarian solutions to the problems of justice. "The balance of forces" thus becomes a critical concept in Niebuhr's analysis of the political evolution of the West.

Pluralism and Class Conflict

Unlike Maritain, Niebuhr was reluctant to give a rational prescription for the just society. His realism caused him to resist all idealistic formulas for organizing the political community. Nevertheless, his writings reveal his loyalty to the historical accomplishments of pluralistic, democratic, and free societies. Though wary of prescriptions, Niebuhr did discover certain "constant prerequisites of free governments." Three such conditions of freedom emerge: "(1) the unity and solidarity of the community, sufficiently strong to allow the free play of competitive interests without endangering the unity of the community itself; (2) a belief in the freedom of the individual and appreciation of his worth; and (3) a tolerable harmony and equilibrium of social and political and economic forces necessary to establish an approximation of social justice."[68]

---

[68]Reinhold Niebuhr and Paul E. Sigmund, *The Democratic Experience: Past and Prospects* (New York: Frederick A. Praeger, 1969) 73.

It is clear that Niebuhr's idea of pluralism included an understanding of the necessity of both diversity and unity, undergirded by the commitment to both liberty and equality. Pluralism is a living experiment in community. It is the pursuit of seemingly incompatible goals: tolerance of diversity *and* solidarity of diverse groups. Niebuhr wrote that democracy, in its ideal form, is a system in which "freedom and order are made to support, not to contradict each other." While there is a necessary conflict between absolute freedom and absolute order, the two demands can be reconciled. "An ideal democratic order seeks unity within the condition of freedom; and maintains freedom within the framework of order."[69]

Pluralist societies consist of myriad institutions and conflicting loyalties—various interest groups contending for a share of power, and various personal loyalties competing within each person. The crucial element in such a pluralistic social system is a vital balance of forces, a creative tension between each legitimate interest. Thus it is important for a free people to understand the social forces involved in each competing interest as well as the political technique of balancing these elements.

A democratic-pluralist society is three systems in one: the political, the economic, and the moral-cultural.[70] Just as the three branches of government in the American polity coexist in an equilibrium of checks and balances, so also do these three systems produce a balance of forces in society at large. Each sector is relatively autonomous. Each has its own rhythms and purposes, which may conflict with the others. Finally, each is subject to the limiting power of the interests represented by the other sectors. Niebuhr dissected and analyzed the conflicts between political, economic, and cultural forces both in periods of depression and in periods of prosperity. Throughout his lifetime he struggled to

---

[69]Reinhold Niebuhr, *The Children of Light and the Children of Darkness: A Vindication of Democracy and a Critique of Its Traditional Defense* (New York: Charles Scribner's Sons, Scribner Library, 1944) 3.

[70]See the discussion of the triune system of democratic pluralism in the section "Mediating Structures and 'Economic Humanism.' "

make the "idea sector"—the moral-cultural sector—relevant to politics and economics. Indeed, Niebuhr showed himself capable of careful discernment as he delineated the various forces and groups that were active in the communal life of modern democracies.

Niebuhr's profound insight into the forces within a pluralist democracy is illustrated by his theory of social class.[71] He found the Marxist formula of owners-versus-workers to be naively simplistic. How could Marxism explain, for example, the differing goals of peasants and the urban protetariat? Niebuhr argues that agrarian groups are better seen as a class in themselves, and that likewise, there is a middle class that is made up of neither owners nor workers. Thus he identifies four major socioeconomic groupings: agrarian, proletarian, capitalist, and middle class. Furthermore, he argued, there are significant distinctions within the middle class: (1) the upper middle class, (2) the managers, (3) the professionals, and (4) the lower middle-class tradesmen and clerks. Differing functions and skills create the conditions of class differentiation. Niebuhr noted a similar distinction in the proletarian class between skilled and unskilled laborers. Thus the Marxist picture of class struggle is partly true, but also partly false, "for it does not do justice to the endless complexity and comparative fluidity of the class structure in democracy."[72]

There are a number of social groupings, then, in a pluralistic society. Each will seek its own interests; none is immune from the temptation to ask more than its due at the expense of others. Pluralism begins with a plurality of social forces. But plurality is not pluralism until the addition of another element: the *balance* of the various forces. How can the conflicting claims of legitimate interest groups be adjudicated and reconciled without plunging society into chaos and anarchy? Naturally, formal techniques such as balloting have their place. Democracy does involve, as an essential component, free elections. But it is much more: it is a social fabric of institutions in creative tension with one another.

---

[71]See Niebuhr, *The Children of Light and the Children of Darkness*, 145-47.

[72]Ibid., 147.

The first step in achieving the required balance is the limitation of the state. Like Maritain, Niebuhr argues that state and society must be understood as distinct but not separate. The state is one institution among others within a society or civilization. Other institutions, such as the church and the family, have their own functions that the state must not impede. The state is charged with a limited task: the maintenance of law and order, the maintenance of a stable currency, and defense against foreign aggression. In these and other matters of the public welfare, the state has an obligation to act. In matters outside its purposes, such as the assignation of religious authority, it has neither the right nor the competence to act. The power of the state is limited in a democratic-pluralist society by a constitution and by laws that guarantee the rights of nongovernmental institutions.

Thus every group, every mediating structure, may exist and defend its liberty of action within its chosen sphere of service. The family serves the common good by nurturing and guiding children and adults to a wholesome and satisfying existence. The church serves the spiritual needs of man and defends his temporal rights. Labor unions and consumer groups represent men and women in the marketplace. Business corporations organize the intellectual and material means of producing wealth. Political parties and movements provide the vehicles for collective decision making. Each and every institution has a place, and should be worthy of its place, within a pluralist society. As human creations, these institutions may succeed or fail in their various tasks; they may become corrupt or exercise overweening power; but they must be preserved, not destroyed. Most important, the balance among them must be maintained.

Niebuhr expresses the ideas of institutional differentiation and the limits of the state in concrete terms. He examines, for example, the emergence of the doctrine of the "consent of the governed" in the early modern era. The distinction between state and society was embodied in the "mutual covenant between king and people," according to which "the king ruled only as long as he obeyed the covenant of justice."[73] The emerging constitutional

---

[73]Niebuhr, *The Structure of Nations and Empires*, 53-54.

monarchy in England became something of a model for democratic experiments around the globe. The idea of the limited state found expression in the writings of John Locke and, in spite of his excessively idealistic confidence in reason, the idea was sufficiently practical to become a vital part of the patrimony of Western democracy. One result of the successful English experiment in self-government was the promulgation of the idea that society extends beyond the boundaries of the state.[74]

The people make up a society through their institutions, and they express their identity through these various social structures. Indeed, some social structures are not "institutions" in the strict sense, but organic groupings below the level of conscious decision making. Niebuhr portrays society as a rich tapestry of forces, institutions, and social structures that affect and are affected by the institutions of government and statecraft.

> Traditional, historical, organic, and natural forces of communal cohesion such as common language, ethnic kinship, geographic factors, common experiences, and common perils . . . operate below the level of conscious decision and bind men together. . . . They create large areas of habitual rather than voluntary association. . . .
>
> The conscious contrivances of statecraft . . . seek to prevent partial and parochial interests from clashing in chaotic competition or conflict, . . . [and to] provide channels for the maximum degree of cooperation.[75]

Niebuhr here emphasizes the different levels of collective self-understanding by which a pluralistic society survives. There are organic and habitual bonds, there are conscious and voluntary associations of all kinds, and there are the rationalized contrivances

---

[74]John Courtney Murray shows how the ideal of "the freedom of the church" operated as a leaven in Western civilization to give rise to notions about the limits of the state and the state's role as servant of society; see his We Hold These Truths, 196-99.

[75]Reinhold Niebuhr, Reinhold Niebuhr on Politics: His Political Philosophy and Its Application to Our Age as Expressed in His Writings, ed. Harry R. Davis and Robert C. Good (New York: Charles Scribner's Sons, 1960) 99.

of statecraft. Each community, each institution, finds its legitimate place within a pluralistic society.

By comparison, the monistic society is organized and regi-
mented from the top down. One power, one elite, and, finally, one
dictator issues the commands in a totalitarian society. The state
seeks to control all other institutions and to absorb society into its
public domain. Family, church, and academy are all subverted by
the political litmus test of party loyalty. The dictatorship of one
class is translated into the rule of its self-proclaimed representative party.

In Soviet Communism, the rigid hierarchy of authority is expressed in the slogan "democratic centralism." No rival grouping
is tolerated outside of state sponsorship and control. Niebuhr
comments on the result of Lenin's revision of Marx in the Soviet
Revolution: "All remnants of the community which opposed [the
party] were but remains of the capitalistic class and had to be liq-
uidated." The various conflicting interests that naturally emerged
in a complex society were suppressed. "The absolute fanaticism,
joined with the absolute utopianism, eliminated all grades and
shades of opinion, so that those who opposed Stalin's enforced
collectivization program were merely defined as " 'Kulaks,' that
is, rich peasants, and were marked for 'liquidation.' "[76] The real
power in the Soviet Union fell increasingly into the hands of the
small clique in the Politburo, and its authority extended to "almost the entire scope of political, economic, social and cultural
problems."[77]

The task of democracy is clear. It consists in "holding all cultural viewpoints under criticism" and "achieving an uncoerced
harmony among the various social and cultural vitalities." "Democracy never gives all the power to the proponents of any one
dogma; it holds all claims to truth under critical review; it balances all social forces, not in an automatic, but in a contrived harmony of power." Groups of all kinds should, says Niebuhr, be held

---

[76]Niebuhr, *The Structure of Nations and Empires*, 228.

[77]Barrington Moore, Jr., *Soviet Politics—The Dilemma of Power* (Cambridge:
Harvard University Press, 1950) 141; quoted ibid., 229.

accountable and purged of their biases by the constant challenge of opposing points of view.[78] A healthy competition of all groups and interests is essential to democratic pluralism. This thesis is elaborated in a particularly vivid way in Niebuhr's treatment of the checks and balances that have emerged in the economic sphere.

Niebuhr on Capitalism and Socialism

The historical evolution of bourgeois democracy is a key theme in Reinhold Niebuhr's thought. His emerging vision of economic justice paralleled the history of the era in which he lived. In his earliest writings, Niebuhr's voice was that of a radical Marxist who predicted an imminent socialist revolution in the United States. Over the course of his long career, Niebuhr came to speak in much more subtle terms of the achievements and deficiencies of "bourgeois democracy." Eventually he offered qualified praise for "capitalistic democracy." John C. Bennett remarks,

> One of the most significant developments in Niebuhr's thought from the 1930's to the 1950's, closely related to the pragmatic method of much of his thought, was his movement away from a dogmatic socialism which was controlled to a considerable extent by the Marxist conception of history. This dogmatic socialism caused him to be almost contemptuous of the New Deal reforms until the late thirties. His confidence in socialism as a total structure dissolved very gradually. . . . The clarification of his doctrine of man . . . the shock from Stalinism, the later attraction of the New Deal revolution and all that it symbolized, and preoccupation with international political problems—all of these factors were present in his movement away from socialism as a system.[79]

---

[78]Niebuhr, Reinhold Niebuhr on Politics, 183-84; Reinhold Niebuhr, Christian Realism and Political Problems (New York: Charles Scribner's Sons, 1953; rpt., Fairfield NJ: Augustus M. Kelley, 1977) 51.

[79]See Harold R. Landon, ed., Reinhold Niebuhr: A Prophetic Voice in Our Time (Greenwich CT: Seabury Press, 1962) 75-76, 86-88.

Niebuhr's break with socialism, although gradual, reached a critical turning point during the late 1930s and early 1940s when Franklin D. Roosevelt's New Deal and Nazism left their marks on history and determined the course of the postmodern world. In 1933 Niebuhr had written, "Capitalism is dying and . . . it ought to die." Throughout the 1930s Niebuhr extolled the virtues of Christian socialism; he was committed to establishing the "highest possible justice" and the "social ownership of the means of production."[80] He and his socialist colleagues at first rejected the New Deal, but by the time of Roosevelt's election to a fourth term, Niebuhr had gradually come to appreciate him. Of course, Roosevelt was preferable to the "big business" candidate, Wendell Wilkie. A "diluted New Deal" was "better than . . . reaction." Besides, Roosevelt had "gone further in progressive domestic policy than any previous President."[81]

On the death of Roosevelt two years later, Niebuhr recorded the significance of the New Deal as the midwife of a truly democratic, politically accountable capitalism: "[Roosevelt] was the first of our political leaders who sought to bring the immense powers of government to bear upon the economic health of the nation and thus to break with the laissez-faire tradition which had a stronger hold upon us than any modern industrial nation."[82] No longer would capitalism be seen as self-regulating; the political accountability of the economic system was established. No longer was socialism the preferred path to a just economic order. On the contrary, socialization of property exposes a nation to a dangerous concentration of power, and creates a "monopoly of power for the oligarchy which manages the socialized property."[83] "The

[80]Reinhold Niebuhr, "After Capitalism—What?" The World Tomorrow 16 (1 March 1933): 203-205; Reinhold Niebuhr, "The Creed of Modern Christian Socialists," Radical Religion 3 (Spring 1938): 13-18.

[81]Reinhold Niebuhr, "A Fourth Term for Roosevelt," The New Statesman and Nation 25 (15 May 1943): 315-16; Reinhold Niebuhr, "Notes," Christianity and Society 8 (Spring 1943): 11.

[82]Reinhold Niebuhr, "The Death of the President," Christianity and Crisis 5 (30 April 1945): 4-6.

[83]Reinhold Niebuhr, "The Anomaly of European Socialism," The Yale Review 42 (December 1952): 161-67.

mistaken ideology of capitalism is not wholly incompatible with the preservation of a free society, while the communist dogma results inevitably in the destruction of freedom."[84]

Niebuhr's appreciation for reformed capitalism ripened in his later life, when he had the opportunity to reflect on decades of political activism. He was searchingly honest about his own past judgments.

> The economic security of the so-called "free" nations is not as established as the proponents of "free enterprise" would have us believe. Nor has perfect justice been established. But it is now perfectly clear that the "capitalistic" culture which was also a democratic one had more moral and political resources to avoid catastrophe than either the Marxists or their Christian fellow travelers believed. . . .
>
> We Christian "prophetic" sympathizers with Marxism were as much in error in understanding the positive program of socialism as we were in sharing its catastrophism.[85]

Capitalism, according to Niebuhr, had managed to reform itself through the tutelage of political democracy. Democratic capitalism provides a realistic view of the distinction between self-interest and self-seeking.

> It was the great achievement of classical economic liberalism to gain recognition of the doctrine that the vast system of mutual services which constitute the life of economic society could best be maintained by relying on the "self interest" of men rather than their "benevolence" or on moral suasion, and by freeing eco-

---

[84]Reinhold Niebuhr, "The World Council of Churches," *Christianity and Society* 13 (Autumn 1948): 3-5.

[85]Reinhold Niebuhr, "Biblical Faith and Socialism: A Critical Appraisal," in *Religion and Culture: Essays in Honor of Paul Tillich*, ed. Walter Leibrecht (New York: Harper & Bros., 1959) 51. In an unpublished letter to D. B. Robertson, dated 3 April 1959, Reinhold Niebuhr wrote, "I do not think the socialist party [in the U.S.] had any significance either in the 20's or the 30's or later, though Norman Thomas has significance for his own personal qualities. I went into the socialist party at that time simply because I had the usual quasi-socialist liberal approach to politics which my whole generation had. I am not too happy about the whole Marxist phase of my career."

nomic activities from irrelevant and frequently undue restrictive political controls.[86]

Furthermore, capitalistic democracy, through the agency of trade unionism, evolved to a point where big business and big labor are "fairly evenly balanced" and have "acquired semi-governmental functions."[87] Here two mediating institutions counterbalance each other in a creative tension, which leads both to a greater sense of public spiritedness and an ethic of service. A new reality has emerged, a democratic capitalism that can produce prosperity *and* equality through the application of incentives and the call to community service.

Bourgeois democracy, said Niebuhr, had greater moral and political resources than he had imagined.

> Bourgeois democracy is rightly regarded in the West as the best form of government because it checks every center of power, and grants no immunity to any form of prestige. . . . Force remained a minimal instrument of government, for the pretensions of any particular government could be challenged in the open society which [the early democratic idealists] created, so that confidence that the government would establish justice was not destroyed. Bourgeois democracy is, therefore, in a more impregnable position, not only in the West but in the world, than are the bourgeois interests which first gave birth to it.[88]

Thus Niebuhr argues that a system of democratic capitalism can solve the problems of economic justice and political self-determination sufficiently to insure its long-term viability. Bourgeois democracy "can achieve a *moral validity* beyond the peculiar conditions which gave it birth."[89]

---

[86]Reinhold Niebuhr, *Faith and Politics: A Commentary on Religious, Social and Political Thought in a Technological Age,* ed. Ronald H. Stone (New York: George Braziller, 1968) 139.

[87]Niebuhr, *Reinhold Niebuhr on Politics,* 223.

[88]Niebuhr, *The Structure of Nations and Empires,* 234-35.

[89]Ibid., 235 (emphasis added).

It would surely not be correct to characterize Niebuhr's entire career as that of a theologian of capitalism. Nevertheless, in his lifelong struggle against the injustices of capitalism, tutored by the experience of the New Deal, Niebuhr developed an allegiance toward a self-reforming and democratized private-enterprise system. Like Maritain, he became one of the first great theorists of democratic capitalism, in spite of, or perhaps because of, his socialist predilections.

Democratic pluralism is the appropriate vehicle, according to Niebuhr, for attaining order and proximate justice in modern societies. Given human sinfulness and selfishness, no other system offers the necessary checks and balances by which human rights are defended and conflicting interests reconciled. The system includes a relative differentiation of powers among the political, the economic, and the cultural sectors. Liberty and equality infuse the political order through the democratic process; they infuse the market economy by rewarding initiative and eliminating special privileges; and they infuse the culture by establishing a free marketplace of ideas, images, and social models. The freedom of each sector is intertwined with the freedom of the others. "Democracy" signifies a social fabric, a living organism, a civilizational experiment in self-government. This ideal underlies all the praise and blame Niebuhr gives to particular historical phenomena. Niebuhr's final judgment on democracy, including capitalistic democracy, is that it is a viable social structure that will continue to prove its moral validity in a world of less-than-perfect political solutions. Niebuhr's vision, like Maritain's, represents a realistic approach to the problems of establishing order and nurturing justice in the political arena. Hence it becomes possible to attempt to describe a theology of freedom that combines the insights and perspectives of both Maritain and Niebuhr—to delineate the convergence of Roman Catholic and Protestant views of the free society.

Converging Visions of Justice

The political life of the Western world today is fundamentally linked to the ideas of democracy and human rights. These two watchwords convey a specific vision, a particular view of individuals and the state. Man is a creature with an inalienable dignity as person, whose destiny transcends temporal existence. Man has rights that are fundamentally beyond the control of the political order: the rights to life and bodily dignity, the freedoms of conscience, faith, and spiritual striving. Every person has a legitimate claim to these rights. There are further rights which all may claim within the social order—for example, the right of legitimate economic pursuit, the rights of family relationship, and of voluntary association for the pursuit of shared interests. Furthermore, every person has a responsibility, insofar as it is possible, to contribute to the establishment of the social order. The principal means to the establishment of this order is the individual in society, in the multitude of interactions that constitute culture. The state is a primary, but by no means the only, instrument for the establishment of the social order. The state is not an end in itself but a tool in the service of collective society and the individual. In a free society the state is established and maintained by democratic consent. Social and political authority, though invested and legitimated in particular institutions and individuals, remains the sole possession of the people as a whole. Personal liberty and self-government are the means and the ends of political life.

This capsule manifesto of democracy and human rights is not unfamiliar to the average Westerner today. It is, as it were, part of the air we breathe. Nevertheless, we are seldom directly aware that these ideas belong to, and are rooted in, the Judeo-Christian tradition. Niebuhr and Maritain help to make us aware of the historical roots of democratic order and justice based on human rights. They also point out the fragility of the institutions and habits of democratic-pluralist life. They both seek a realistic understanding and a proximate realization of democracy and human rights. My comparison of the content of these two political theologies reveals striking agreements and provocative complementarities. The political theories of Maritain and Niebuhr each center on the common good, the dignity and responsibility of the person, and the social ideal of democratic pluralism. Yet there are differences in style and in intellectual lineage.

For Niebuhr, as for Maritain, politics is a branch of ethics. The political order must be judged in reference to moral criteria, which exist in relation to spiritual imperatives. The goal of political prudence and justice is to serve the common good; the Christian seeks prudence and a justice infused by love. Maritain emphasizes the necessarily instrumental role of the state in serving the common good of the body of politic, and the obligation of each person and each nation to serve and to seek the common good of global civilization. Niebuhr emphasizes the shared destiny of the pluralistic community, which calls for a unity and solidarity made possible by a vision of freedom and the common good. For both Maritain and Niebuhr, only that which serves the common good possesses genuine political authority; government is intrinsically authoritative when it is truly representative of a people, not when it simply exercises "sovereignty" in the land.[90]

Niebuhr emphasizes the necessity of a balance of power to achieve the common good; Maritain emphasizes the need for mutual cooperation. In either case, the fundamental need is for the free society to enjoy a real measure of communal solidarity, fraternity, and civic friendship. These qualities can never be imposed from above by the state because civic faith is a possession of the people; it properly belongs to the body politic, not the state per se. The instrumentalist theory of the state, elaborated by Maritain and Niebuhr alike, stands in direct opposition to absolutist or totalitarian theories in which the state claims to directly embody communal solidarity, to constitute a "superman" or "collective will." Thus Maritain and Niebuhr were ardent opponents of Communist hegemony and critics of statism within any system of government. The common good, which is the aim of politics, belongs to the people, not to the state.

Maritain and Niebuhr reflect their distinct traditions of Roman Catholicism and Protestantism, respectively, in their concepts of human nature. Their formulation of a Christian anthropology comes from two distinct intellectual traditions. Nevertheless, they set forth similar theses regarding the sublime

---

[90]See, e.g., Maritain, *Man and the State*, ch. 2: "The Concept of Sovereignty."

worth of the individual, his political rights, privileges, and obligations, and his relation to the body politic through an intrinsic civic faith. The person has worldly dignity and a destiny beyond the temporal ends of the political order. Within the political order, the person possesses inalienable rights to a *qualified* self-determination in social, political, and economic life (qualified because no absolutely perfect reconciliation of interests is possible in the temporal sphere). Individual liberty and equality of opportunity must not be abridged. Yet individual liberty must be balanced against collective solidarity. Each person is a valued whole in relation to other valued wholes.

Political man achieves a tolerable measure of justice through the exercise of his capacities of practical wisdom and realism. Maritain and Niebuhr agree on this point. Niebuhr emphasizes the sinfulness of man, the evils that result from his self-delusion regarding his own righteousness and the righteousness of his cause, and the tragic fact that freedom is the locus of both human weakness and strength. For Niebuhr, there is always a paradoxical *tension* between love and justice that makes the solution of political problems a process of realistic self-criticism and paradoxical insight. By contrast, Maritain emphasizes the potentiality of the person for rational and virtuous action, the universal drive toward the good, and the possibilities for expressions of practical wisdom uncorrupted by ideological reductionism. There is, for Maritain, an analogical *harmony* between love and prudence, and a unity of the virtues of prudence, justice, courage, and temperance. The solution to the political problem lies in the prudent application of rational principles and analogical insights.

For Maritain *and* for Niebuhr, a person exercises his political responsibility when the virtues of love, justice, and prudence operate within him to bring about the conservation and transformation of political culture. Every political structure must change as it advances toward the goal of the common good. It must also maintain hard-won advances toward justice. For example, history has decreed a new status for the working class within the modern balance of social forces—a status championed by both Maritain and Niebuhr. The economic rights won by the bourgeoisie were necessarily broadened to include the rights of the wage workers. The case is exemplary. The dignity of the person and his vision of the common good demand the continuing transformation of the existing structures of power.

Personal dignity and human rights are a prominent aspect of the political philosophies of Maritain and Niebuhr. But Maritain was more inclined than Niebuhr to believe that a global consensus on human rights and the beginnings of a legitimate, global political authority were possible. Niebuhr was more pessimistic about the ability of democratic pluralism, with its commitment to human rights, to encircle the globe. Both men struggled for this end. Both viewed history as open-ended; and both believed in the personalist vision of human agency building a just social order. Maritain and Niebuhr present a dialectical view of the person as an intelligent, willful, and responsible locus of political participation.

Liberty and the equality of persons must be complemented, according to Maritain and Niebuhr, by the fraternity that makes social cohesion possible. Political society demands some measure of friendship or civic faith between citizens who consider themselves equals. This involves a view of the common good that acknowledges the contributions to society made by each person and each institution, even when they operate in competitive relationships. This necessary measure of fraternity occurs whenever the people share a common civic faith in certain fundamental principles: "truth and intelligence, human dignity, freedom, brotherly love, and the absolute value of moral good."[91]

In our time these principles of civic faith are embodied in systems of democratic pluralism. Authority is extended and checked democratically, through the participation of individual persons in the process of representational self-government. There is a balance between individual and collective demands. In a democracy there is a plurality of interests and powers, balanced according to the principles of respect for the person and service to the common good. Every ethnic group, every subculture, has a rightful share in the plurality of power. Mutual toleration does not contradict true

---

[91]Ibid., 111.

cultural fidelity, since it is out of the diversity of a nation that its unity develops. True freedom and order coexist in such a system.

Both Maritain and Niebuhr argue that the primary laboratories of political participation and societal transformation are democratic-pluralist societies. Similarly, they see the very negation of these ideals manifested in totalitarian societies. Both men warn of the serious threat to civilization posed by totalitarianism and statism in all its forms, and at the same time they applaud democratic pluralism for partially solving the problems of power and authority.

Maritain and Niebuhr elaborate a remarkably similar defense of democratic pluralism and human rights in their respective political theologies. Each offers a realistic and morally engaged understanding of the political order. The specific content of political theory in Maritain and Niebuhr is often almost identical. What distinguishes them are the styles of moral reflection, the inherited languages, the controlling images of their philosophical systems. But even here, close examination reveals not opposition but complementarity.

Two Types
of Political Theology

> The Christians of the center . . . cannot separate the works of human culture from the grace of God, for all those works are possible only by grace. But neither can they separate the experience of grace from cultural activity; for how can men love the unseen God in response to His love without serving the visible brother in human society?

> H. Richard Niebuhr
> Christ and Culture[1]

[1](New York: Harper & Row, Harper Torchbooks, 1956) 119.

V

The conventional wisdom of the contemporary Western world assumes that politics and religion are separate realms of human concern—one concerned with the practical day-to-day problems and needs of life in community, the other devoted to speculation about an ultimate purpose and meaning in the universe. The problem lies in the way the two realms are seen as not merely distinct but *separate*—as if the day-to-day needs of human life could have no connection with the possibility of an ultimate human purpose devolving from a source of truth.

Recent history has discredited the concept of the separation of politics and religion. Politico-religious wars and revolutions in various countries, the increasingly important role of religious groups in democratic elections, the debates over evolution, abortion, and human rights—all in particular ways illustrate the close connections between political man and *homo religiosus*. All of these examples underscore the wisdom of traditional Christian attempts to achieve a theoretical synthesis of the natural and the supernatural ends of humankind.

We find ourselves today in the same situation as Aquinas when he accepted the challenge of assimilating to Christian philosophy the ideas he found in the rediscovered manuscripts of Aristotle. In Aristotle he discovered a perfect exposition of the *natural* ends of human existence, an exposition waiting for the completion that a thorough analysis of the *supernatural* ends would provide. As in Aquinas's time, Christian political theology can provide the contemporary world with tools for assessing the interplay of natural and supernatural ends.

Jacques Maritain and Reinhold Niebuhr provide two distinct but complementary solutions, two political theologies, that explicitly address this problem of the relationship of politics and religion. There are, of course, other possible solutions. In simplest terms, the political realm and the spiritual realm can be understood to be either fundamentally discontinuous or fundamentally continuous. One can think of the possible ways of relating the two realms as a spectrum from discontinuity to continuity. At one end is the style of Christian political theology characterized by withdrawal from participation in the dominant political culture and the erection of an ethical wall between the realms of religion and politics. One thinks of the Radical Reformers of the sixteenth and seventeenth centuries and the political theology of Leo Tolstoy. At the opposite end of the spectrum is a style characterized by the affirmation of coinciding religious and cultural values; the highest political and cultural ideals are viewed as perfectly compatible with, even identical to, the highest religious ideals. Prominent examples of this style are Abelard, John Locke, and Immanuel Kant.[2]

---

[2]Many readers will note here and throughout this chapter a heavy debt to H. Richard Niebuhr's landmark study, *Christ and Culture.* He establishes a five-fold typology ranging from "Christ against culture" (oppositionist) to "Christ of culture" (accommodationist) and including "Christ and culture in paradox" (dualist), "Christ above culture" (synthetic), and—the central position—"Christ transforming culture" (conversionist). While identifying himself with the conversionist style, H. Richard Niebuhr, in a now famous footnote, identifies his brother, Reinhold, as a dualist. He identifies the traditional Roman Catholic approach as synthetic.

Two additional significant attempts to sketch a typology of Christian political thought deserve mention. Dante L. Germino's "Two Types of Recent Chris-

Clearly, neither Maritain nor Niebuhr can be identified with the styles at either end of the spectrum. In fact, they both point out the dangers of either extreme. Yet they each express appreciation for the contributions made to the Christian tradition of political theology by conceptual styles across the entire spectrum. They even employ in their writings themes from the whole spectrum. Still, certain tendencies can be clearly identified for each of them. In general, Maritain tends to emphasize the continuity between the spiritual and temporal realms, while Niebuhr emphasizes their discontinuity.

These contrasting styles—I have called Maritain's style *analogic* and Niebuhr's *paradoxic*—manifest a complementarity of opposites. The political theologies of Maritain and Niebuhr are distinct; their Roman Catholic and Protestant orientations clearly differ. Yet their practical conclusions converge at the point of describing a social order that protects human rights through the institutions of democratic pluralism. Through the use of opposite controlling metaphors, they arrive at similar models of social order.

Maritain's Analogic Approach

Natural law is a subordinate extension of the divine law of God. The former reveals to man his temporal end or goal, and the latter reveals his supernatural end. This fundamental vision of a connected hierarchy of the two realms of religion and politics is central to Maritain's social philosophy. Maritain sees the two realms in an analogic relationship—dissimilar with respect to their ontological referents, similar with respect to their source. I have already discussed the importance of this hierarchy for

---

tian Political Thought," *The Journal of Politics* 21 (August 1959): 455-86, compares the "rationalist" and "fideist" approaches. According to Germino, prominent representatives of the former type are Jacques Maritain and Yves Simon; the latter type includes Reinhold Niebuhr, Karl Barth, and Emil Brunner. The other significant typology analyzes only the Protestant tradition; it is Thomas G. Sanders's *Protestant Concepts of Church and State: Historical Backgrounds and Approaches for the Future* (New York: Holt, Rinehart & Winston, 1964; rpt., Garden City NY: Doubleday & Co., Anchor Books, 1965). Sanders partially adopts H. Richard Niebuhr's typology, labeling both Niebuhr brothers as "transformationists" (24).

distinguishing between theoretical wisdom and practical wisdom. I am now interested in the implications of this analogic approach for problems of church and state and political theology in general.

Maritain was devoted throughout his intellectual life to carefully maintaining the distinction between the things that are Caesar's and the things that are God's. His first major political treatise, *La Primauté du spirituel*, was published in English under the title *The Things That Are Not Caesar's*.[3] In that book Maritain attempts to illustrate the relationship between reason and truth, the human and the divine. "The fact is that the order of reason, no longer kept within the order of charity, has everywhere disintegrated and is no longer good for anything." He is here decrying the "rationalist evil" that has attempted to sever the lower realm of nature from the supernatural. "A man must place his stake either above reason and still for it, or below reason and against it. But only the theological virtues and the supernatural gifts and infused contemplation are above reason." Clearly, the cardinal virtues of prudence, justice, courage, and temperance cannot manifest themselves without the theological virtues of faith, hope, and charity. "Wherever the living faith takes root, there we shall see the adhesion to what is truly above reason, to uncreated Truth and the wisdom of the saints, simultaneously achieve—assuredly not without labor—the restoration of the very order of reason, implied as a condition for supernatural life." He concludes with a typical expression of the analogic world view: "And so the Gospel and philosophy, mystic and metaphysician, divine and human go hand in hand."[4]

Maritain's references to the two realms are found throughout his political and theological writings. He is particularly precise in outlining the differences between the civil society of the state and

---

[3]Trans. J. F. Scanlan (London: Sheed & Ward, 1930).

[4]Jacques Maritain, *The Social and Political Philosophy of Jacques Maritain: Selected Readings*, ed. Joseph W. Evans and Leo R. Ward (New York: Charles Scribner's Sons, 1955, rpt., Notre Dame IN: University of Notre Dame Press, 1976) 148-49.

the supratemporal society of the church. Man, according to Maritain, achieves his very being and identity in social groups. He is a social animal, as Aristotle taught. But, while society is natural to human persons, there is a higher calling to which man should aspire. "The ultimate end of man is not society, but God."[5] Thus, Maritain explains, there is always an uneasy relationship between the individual and the group.

> There will always exist a certain tension between person and society. This paradox, this tension, this conflict are themselves something both natural and inevitable. Their solution is not static, it is dynamic; it provokes movement and is accomplished in movement. . . . Thus the person craves society, and tends always to surpass it, until Man enters at last into the society of God.[6]

Maritain describes the various planes of existence or societies in which a person realizes his identity and purpose. The first society is the family, followed by voluntary associations of free individuals with various shared interests and concerns. Then comes the civil society or body politic, which incorporates all these interests in its defense of the common good. Finally, there is the society of God-related souls, persons seeking their supernatural end. "Above the plane of civil society, the person crosses the threshold of a kingdom which is *not of this world* and enters a supranational, supra-racial, supra-temporal society which is called the Church."[7]

Maritain defines "four characteristics of a society of free men."[8] It is *personalist* because it respects the dignity of the individuals who constitute the group. It is *communal* because it places the common good above individual interests. It is *pluralist* because it defends the right of the person to participate in various autono-

---

[5]Jacques Maritain, *The Rights of Man and Natural Law*, trans. Doris C. Anson (New York: Charles Scribner's Sons, 1943; rpt., New York: Gordian Press, 1971) 18-19.

[6]Ibid.

[7]Ibid., 19.

[8]Ibid., subheading, 20.

mous communities. And, finally, it is *theist* or *Christian* because it recognizes God as the "source of natural law" and the "end of the human person."

Free society does not require each member to believe in God or to be a Christian; it recognizes that some will not. It even expects the unbelieving member to make a positive contribution to justice and the common good. But it is not a society that denies God or ignores its own ground of being in the supernatural.

> Civil society is organically linked to religion and turns consciously towards the source of its being by invoking divine assistance and the divine name as its members know it. Independent in its own temporal sphere, it has above it the kingdom of things that are not Caesar's, and it must cooperate with religion, not by any kind of theocracy or clericalism, nor by exercising any sort of pressure in religious matters, but by respecting and facilitating, on the basis of the rights and liberties of each of us, the spiritual activity of the Church and of the diverse religious families which are grouped within the temporal community.[9]

It is difficult to find a more forceful expression than this of the Thomistic vision in contemporary theological discourse.

Maritain's approach holds Christ above culture, religion above politics, and church above state. But it does affirm the relative autonomy of the lower realm. There is an analogic relationship between the two realms in which the lower is subordinate to the higher. Moreover, it is a dynamic relationship: the political virtues, such as prudence and justice, are perfected by the theological virtue of love. Similarly, for Reinhold Niebuhr, the perfection of justice is found in love, though he more firmly emphasizes the tension or paradox between these two virtues and two realms.

Having suggested the positive side—Maritain's view of the ideal relationship of the two realms—it is appropriate to examine his negative judgments concerning certain alternative approaches to the question of the two realms. These he discusses under the rubric of "three errors" with regard to the "problem of

---

[9]Ibid., 22.

the kingdom of God."[10] The "problem" concerns the proper relationship of the Kingdom of God, the church, and the world. Given the distinction between the spiritual and the temporal, what is the meaning of the world and of the church in relation to the eschatological goal of the Kingdom of God? Maritain notes that the idea of the church is distinct from the idea of the Kingdom of God. There is not, however, an utter opposition between the two. The clue is found in the dynamics of God's redemptive plan. "The Church is the kingdom of God begun. . . . But it is not the kingdom of God in its state of *definitive realization.*" Maritain calls the church the "chrysalis" of the Kingdom of God; it is "in a state of pilgrimage."[11] With the problem thus stated, Maritain moves on to discuss three errors in understanding the relationship of world, church, and Kingdom of God. The first error assumes a too radical separation of the world and the Kingdom of God, while the second and third errors go to the other extreme of theocratic and anthropocentric utopianism.

The first error, says Maritain, "consists in making of the world and of the earthly city purely and simply the kingdom of Satan. . . . It is what we may call a *satanocratic* conception of the world and of the political city." This radical separation of the two realms ends finally in the denial of the salvation of the world and the abandonment of nature, and it "restricts redemption to the invisible empire of souls and to the moral order."[12] Maritain boldly identifies tendencies in this direction in the thought of certain early Christians (he is perhaps referring to Tertullian), the Protestant Reformers, Machiavelli, Descartes, and Karl Barth. But Maritain is careful to condemn only certain tendencies of thought while reserving judgment on individual theologians.

The second error is described by Maritain as *theocratic.* It is a form of utopianism. "Not only is the world saved in hope, but [the

---

[10]Jacques Maritain, *Integral Humanism: Temporal and Spiritual Problems of a New Christendom,* trans. Joseph W. Evans (New York: Charles Scribner's Sons, 1968; rpt., Notre Dame IN: University of Notre Dame Press, 1973) 99-111.

[11]Ibid., 101n, 102.

[12]Ibid., 103.

theocrat] believes that it is necessary—to the extent that the work of redemption takes place in it—that in its temporal existence itself it appear as already really and fully saved—as the kingdom of God." The mistake here is to deny Jesus' statement that his kingdom is "not of this world." This view is contrary to the belief that "Christ did not come to change the kingdoms of the earth or to accomplish a temporal revolution."[13] Maritain cites as examples certain tendencies or temptations in Eastern Christendom, including Russian Orthodoxy (Dostoevski's *Legend of the Grand Inquisitor*), Western Christendom, Calvinism, the Counter-Reformation, and the Spanish monarchy. A "progressively more secular" version of this error is found in Hegelianism and Marxism, in which a sacred mission is assigned to the state or class.[14] Again, Maritain is criticizing only certain tendencies or temptations without passing judgment on individual thinkers.

The third error, according to Maritain, "consists in seeing in the world and in the terrestrial city purely and simply the domain of man and of pure nature, without any relationship either to the sacred or a supernatural destiny, or to God or the devil." This "anthropocentric humanism" is exemplified in the work of Auguste Comte, with his secularized view of the Kingdom of God—a view that contributed as well to the error of Marxism already cited. The fault of this approach lies in denying the gospel message that there is a higher purpose in human life, the message that "man does not live by bread alone, but by every word that comes forth from the mouth of God."[15]

Having rejected both the radical separation and the uncritical identification of the two realms, Maritain turns to what he considers the orthodox Christian solution. He stresses the essential "ambiguity of the world and its history." The world is a dynamic process moving toward both salvation and damnation, which "belongs to God by right of creation; to the devil by right of conquest because of sin; to Christ by right of victory over the con-

---

[13]Ibid., 104-105.

[14]Ibid., 106-107.

[15]Ibid., 107-108, quoting Deut. 8:3, Matt. 4:4, and Luke 4:4.

queror, because of the passsion." The Christian has one task in the world: "to dispute with the devil his domain, to wrest it from him; he must strive to this end, he will succeed in it only in part as long as time will endure."[16] Thus, for Maritain, the world is an ambivalent realm, a place where good and evil grow together, like the wheat and the tares in Jesus' parable, until the end of time.

Maritain describes an analogic relationship of the spiritual and the temporal. They are held in a permanent, dynamic, and redemptive tension. They are alike yet dissimilar; and their ultimate end lies beyond history in the hands of God. Here again there is a deep affinity with the paradoxic approach of Reinhold Niebuhr.

In *Man and the State*, Maritain describes the relationship between church and state in terms of three "general immutable principles." Each of these principles illustrates one aspect of the relationship between church and state, and by implication, between religion and politics. The first principle is "*the freedom of the church to teach and preach and worship, the freedom of the Gospel, the freedom of the word of God.*"[17] This principle suggests the need for a certain degree of separation between the two realms. The church has its own distinct authority to minister to the supernatural ends of man without interference from the state. The freedom of the church derives from the right of association, the right of religious belief, and the freedom of God himself vis-à-vis any human institution.

The second principle is "*the superiority of the church—that is, of the spiritual—over the body politic or the State.*" This principle implies the relative autonomy of the state to concern itself with the temporal, common good, and not to have this prerogative usurped by clerical authorities. Furthermore, this principle maintains the superiority of spiritual values over temporal values, the perfecting of the latter by the former, and the superiority of the church "in her essence" over "every body politic."[18]

---

[16]Ibid., 108-109.

[17]Jacques Maritain, *Man and the State* (Chicago: University of Chicago Press, Phoenix Books, 1951) 151-52.

[18]Ibid., 152-53.

The third principle is "*the necessary cooperation between the church and the body politic or the State.*" Religion and politics, church and state, must interact and enable each other to fulfill their respective purposes. Maritain argued that it is possible to do this without imposing any form of theocracy, clericalism, or coercion in religious matters. Such cooperation is necessary because "the human person is simultaneously a member of [the church and] that society which is the body politic."[19]

In the last analysis, for Maritain, there is an analogic resemblance and distinction between the world and the Kingdom of God. On the one hand, "there is . . . an 'ontosophic truth' about the world considered in its natural structures or in what properly constitutes it; in this sense we must say that the world is fundamentally good." Yet when the world swallows up all memory of the other world of the Heavenly Father and fails to distinguish itself from the Kingdom of God, all is lost. "There is a 'religious' or 'mystical' truth about the world considered in its ambiguous relationship to the Kingdom of God and Incarnation. . . . It is the *adversary* of Christ and his disciples, and *hates* them."[20] Both truths are crucial, says Maritain, for the right ordering of the relationship of the two realms. Without both the continuity and the discontinuity, the analogic relationship between religion and politics breaks down: Christ is either too far above culture to save it or not above it at all, as if it were already saved.

Niebuhr's Paradoxic Approach

What is the relation of religion to politics, according to Niebuhr? His general theme is "the moral tension between Christ and the world" or the "tension of love and justice."[21] Ambiguity, ten-

---

[19]Ibid., 153-54.

[20]Jacques Maritain, *The Peasant of the Garonne: An Old Layman Questions Himself About the Present Time,* trans. Michael Cuddihy and Elizabeth Hughes (New York: Holt, Rinehart & Winston, 1968; rpt., New York: Macmillan Co., 1969) 75.

[21]Reinhold Niebuhr, *Faith and Politics: A Commentary on Religious, Social and Political Thought in a Technological Age,* ed. Ronald H. Stone (New York: George Braziller, 1968) 38-39.

sion, conflict, and paradox are the terms by which he discusses the problem of the two realms. Yet in spite of his emphasis on the discontinuities of the two realms, he does not conceive of religion and politics as wholly separate or ultimately irreconcilable. "The Christian doctrine of creation does not set the eternal and divine into absolute contradiction to the temporal and the historical."[22] There is a paradox between the eternal and the temporal that makes perfect love a historical impossibility and an inevitable eschatological necessity. For Niebuhr, politics is a project for achieving proximate justice, the kind that reflects the higher law of love symbolized by Christ's sacrifice.

Niebuhr frequently describes his "Christian realist" approach as one that avoids the two erroneous extremes of political theology that are embodied in Christian liberalism and Christian orthodoxy, respectively. The former, he argues, takes a too optimistic view of the relationship between religion and politics, and the latter a too pessimistic view. "The relation of Christianity to the problems of politics and economics has not been a particularly fortunate or inspiring one." Niebuhr notes, however, that this statement is not unqualified; Thomist and Calvinist contributions to political theory are "obvious exceptions." Yet, ironically, secular rationalism has contributed more to solving the problem of justice than has Christianity. "Among the many possible causes of this failure of Christianity in politics the most basic is the tendency of Christianity to destroy the dialectic of prophetic religion, either by sacrificing time and history to eternity or by giving ultimate significance to the relativities of history." Because of its "undue pessimism," says Niebuhr, nineteenth- and twentieth-century Christian orthodoxy chose the first alternative; and because of its "undue sentimentality," Christian liberalism chose the second.[23]

---

[22]Reinhold Niebuhr, *The Nature and Destiny of Man*, 2 vols. (New York: Charles Scribner's Sons, Scribner Library, 1941-1943) 2:96.

[23]Reinhold Niebuhr, *An Interpretation of Christian Ethics* (New York: Harper & Bros., 1935; rpt., New York: Meridian Books, Living Age Books, 1956) 128-29.

> In the one case [orthodoxy] the fact of the "sinfulness of the world"
> was used as an excuse for the complacent acceptance of whatever
> imperfect justice a given social order had established. . . . In the
> other case [liberalism] the problems of politics were approached
> from the perspective of a sentimental moralism and with no un-
> derstanding for either the mechanistic and amoral factors in so-
> cial life or the mechanical and technical prerequisites of social
> justice.[24]

Like Maritain, Niebuhr calls for a solution to the problem that
avoids either the separation or complete identification of the two
realms. His specific purpose is to expose the tendencies toward
these extremes in both the Christian right and the Christian left in
the twentieth century. His critique is still relevant for Christians
involved in politics today.

Like Maritain, Niebuhr criticized the utopianism of those who
felt that it was possible to realize perfect justice in the social order. And both theologians criticized as well those who had de-
spaired of trying. Niebuhr wrote, "Men always jump to the
erroneous conclusion that because they can conceive of a truth and
a justice that completely transcends their interests, they are therefore also able to realize such truth and such justice. Against this
error of the optimists, Protestant pessimism affirms the equally
absurd proposition that sin has completely destroyed all truth and
justice." Yet there is something positive in each side as well, as
long as the viewpoints are not made absolute. "Protestant pessimism is but a corrupted form of a prophetic criticism which
Christianity must make even against its own culture."[25] Men are
corrupted, as Protestant pessimism emphasizes, but they are also
potential agents of love.

> Men are not completely blinded by self-interest or lost in this maze
> of historical relativity. . . . What remains with them is . . . the law
> of love, which they dimly recognize as the law of their being, as

---

[24]Ibid., 129.

[25]Reinhold Niebuhr, Love and Justice: Selections from the Shorter Writings
of Reinhold Niebuhr, ed. D. B. Robertson (Philadelphia: Westminster Press, 1957;
rpt., Gloucester MA: Peter Smith, 1976) 51.

the structure of human freedom. . . . It is the weakness of Protestant pessimism that it denies the reality of this potential perfection and its relevance in the affairs of politics.[26]

Niebuhr is careful to explain both sides of his paradox. Politics is the art of achieving proximate justice, not utopia. Political man is capable of justice and even some acts of love, but he remains partially blinded by his own pride and self-interest. The paradox of religion and politics is permanent in history. The resolution of the paradox is an eschatological hope.

Niebuhr always discusses the state in a way that emphasizes the coexistence within it of justice and injustice. The tension or paradox between the two realms is implied by his frequent references to the "moral ambiguities of government." The biblical message concerning government, he argues, contains two themes that must be "taken together and held in balance." On the one hand, "government is an ordinance of God and its authority reflects the Divine Majesty." On the other hand, "the 'rulers' and 'judges' of the nations are particularly subject to divine judgment and wrath because they oppress the poor and defy the divine majesty."[27]

Thus, in the biblical attitude toward government, there is a dual approach, which is both critical and responsible. Only a political theology that retains both elements can be consistent with the whole message of the Bible. Those who "came closest to a full comprehension of all the complexities of political justice" were those who "freed the religious conscience from undue reverence for any particular government and established a critical attitude toward it, while yet preserving religious reverence for the principle of government."[28]

Politics, and by implication the state, is morally ambiguous because of the permanent factors of self-interest and power which must be controlled, but cannot be eliminated, in the social order.

---

[26]Ibid., 53.

[27]Niebuhr, The Nature and Destiny of Man, 2:269.

[28]Ibid., 2:281-82.

For Niebuhr, the political world is not, and cannot be, the Kingdom of God. "Politics always aims at some kind of a harmony or balance of interest, and such a harmony cannot be regarded as directly related to the final harmony of love of the Kingdom of God." There are two distinct realms, a realm of proximate justice and a realm of pure love, and they are related only indirectly. Niebuhr emphasizes the distinction by saying "the first duty of Christian faith is to preserve a certain distance between the sanctities of faith and the ambiguities of politics."[29]

Niebuhr's most complete expression of the ambiguity of politics and the state is found in his treatment of the love ethic in politics. He calls the law of love a paradox, "a law and yet not a law." Because the essential character of love is that it "desires the good freely and without compulsion," it cannot be enforced like a law— "it is a norm but not an obligation." The notion of enforcing or coercing love is self-contradictory. "The law of love therefore presupposes a human personality which is not at war with itself, that is, a sinless soul." But men's souls are not without sin. "Thus the paradox in a simple commandment, 'Thou shalt love' . . . is a faithful expression of the basic paradox of all human morality."[30] Because of the fundamental corruption of all human morality, the morality of persons involved in political communities necessarily falls short of perfection. Even the highest achievements of human law and the most equitable balancing of opposing interests will be only tentative, relative, and approximate. The law of love will always remain a standard beyond historical realization, one that demands a deeper justice. The cross, according to Niebuhr, will always symbolize the sacrificial love that transcends history and relativizes all human attempts at justice.[31]

The moral ambiguity of politics and the state has definite implications, in Niebuhr's view, for the relationship of church and

---

[29]Reinhold Niebuhr, Reinhold Niebuhr on Politics: His Political Philosophy and Its Application to Our Age as Expressed in His Writings, ed. Harry R. Davis and Robert C. Good (New York: Charles Scribner's Sons, 1960) 193-94.

[30]Ibid., 134.

[31]Niebuhr, The Nature and Destiny of Man, 2:68.

state. Niebuhr notes a tendency in Roman Catholicism to confuse the Kingdom of God with the historical church. This is precisely the problem that Maritain warned against when he said that the church is the Kingdom of God *begun*, but not its *definitive realization*. The first principle of the church-state relation for Niebuhr, as for Maritain, is to avoid equating the church with any particular political movement or state. Niebuhr writes, "The Catholic church tends to identify the historic church with the Kingdom of God, and too often its final criterion is what a political movement promises or does not promise to the historic church." He further warns against the practice of sanctioning religious political parties and uncritically defending the so-called "Christian state." Nevertheless, for Niebuhr, the Catholic faith has made important contributions to democratic-pluralist societies, including the United States. "Most American non-Catholics have a very inaccurate concept of Roman Catholic political thought and life." It is not a tradition of authoritarianism, as some misinformed American Protestants believe. Non-Roman Catholics "underestimate the resources of Catholicism for preserving justice and stability in a free society, once established."[32]

Elsewhere, in a more general context, Niebuhr rejects all attempts, whether Roman Catholic or Protestant, to yoke religion and politics. He warns against the denigration of the sanctity of the church that would come about as a result of being identified with morally ambiguous political movements.

> When the sanctification of the Church is extended to the sanctification of political programs, movements, or systems, the baneful effects are compounded. One need not be a secularist to believe that politics in the name of God is of the devil. This should be obvious to right-minded religious people, for religious politics invariably gives an ultimate sanction to highly ambiguous political programs. Every political policy, however justified, must be regarded as ambiguous when related to the ultimate sanctity.[33]

---

[32]Niebuhr, *Reinhold Niebuhr on Politics*, 203-204.

[33]Ibid., 203.

Ambiguity, tension, and paradox are the operative metaphors in Niebuhr's discussion of the two realms. They are especially useful guides in understanding the relationship between religious and political institutions. Neither Roman Catholicism, Protestantism, nor any other type of Christian belief is immune from the possibility of a "dangerous alliance between religion and power." Confusion of the two realms is, in fact, a "perennial factor" in all human history.[34] Islamic society, Niebuhr notes in passing, has been constantly tempted toward an uncritical theocracy, in spite of the prophetic element in the message conveyed through Muhammad.[35] "Theocratic utopianism," as Maritain called it, is a persistent heresy. It is condemned by Niebuhr as well.

What, then, should be the practical approach to preserving this necessary distinction between church and state? For Maritain and Niebuhr, the answer lies in finding creative solutions. There is even a possibility, they argue, that *cooperation* between church and state does not preclude *separation* of church and state. Niebuhr's discussion of state aid to parochial schools is illustrative. "Our constitutional fathers quite obviously and quite rightly wanted to prevent the establishment of religious monopoly." But it is "not at all clear that they sought to prevent the state's support of religion absolutely, provided such support could be given equitably to all religious groups." On the one hand, it may be difficult to meet these conditions given the degree of America's "religious heterogeneity." But, on the other hand, the issue should not be prematurely settled according to the strictest standard of separation. The principle of "complete separation is a valuable heritage; but no one can deny that the price we pay for it is the official secularization of our culture."[36]

---

[34]Ibid., 204-205.

[35]See Reinhold Niebuhr, *The Structure of Nations and Empires: A Study of the Recurring Patterns and Problems of the Political Order in Relation to the Unique Problems of the Nuclear Age* (New York: Charles Scribner's Sons, 1959; rpt., Fairfield NJ: Augustus M. Kelley, 1977) 115-18.

[36]Niebuhr, *Reinhold Niebuhr on Politics*, 205.

Thus there is a similarity between Maritain and Niebuhr concerning their practical viewpoints on the church-state relation. There is, as well, a perception shared by Maritain and Niebuhr of the dangers of either utterly divorcing or completely uniting the two realms. Finally, their views are close with regard to the value of alternative styles of political theology.

In a provocative passage, Niebuhr defends the contributions of martyrs, prophets, and statesmen, suggesting their value in relation to the several styles of Christian political theology.

> Martyrs, prophets and statesmen may each in his own way be servants of the Kingdom. Without the martyr we might live under the illusion that the kingdom of Caesar is the Kingdom of Christ in embryo and forget that there is a fundamental contradiction between the two kingdoms. Without the successful prophet, whose moral indictments effect actual changes in the world, we might forget that each moment of human history faces actual and realizable higher possibilities. Without the statesman, who uses power to correct the injustices of power, we might allow the vision of the Kingdom of Christ to become a luxury of those who can afford to acquiesce in present injustice because they do not suffer from it.[37]

No other passage in Niebuhr's writings better summarizes his appreciation for the variety of styles of relating religion and politics. Yet Niebuhr clearly emphasizes the paradoxic approach even as he acknowledges the contributions of each of the traditional approaches to the problem of the two realms. Niebuhr reminds us of the tension and ambiguity between the spiritual and the temporal, and he reminds us of our dual obligation to seek justice and to perfect it through love.

Complementary Opposites

Most strands of the tradition of Christian political theology— except those at either extreme of the spectrum—acknowledge the complexity of the relations between religion and politics. Each al-

---

[37]Reinhold Niebuhr, *Beyond Tragedy: Essays on the Christian Interpretation of History* (New York: Charles Scribner's Sons, The Scribner Library, 1937) 286.

lows some distinction, and some relation, between the grace of God and the works of culture. So it is with the theologies of Maritain and Niebuhr. Maritain, an analogic thinker, traces out careful definitions of world, church, and Kingdom of God. He sees the relationship of the two realms as hierarchical, with grace perfecting natural law. His controlling metaphor is the *analogy* of Christ and culture, with Christ in the superior position. Niebuhr, on the other hand, leans toward a nonhierarchical, discontinuous relationship between the two realms. There is tension, ambiguity, and conflict between the morally flawed realm of power, interests, and selfishness and a morally absolute Divine Being. Niebuhr's controlling metaphor is the *paradox* between Christ and culture.

Both thinkers advocate a careful separation of the institutions of church and state; but both suggest limited forms of cooperation as well. The church-state problem has been a perennial source of confusion, according to Maritain and Niebuhr, which has made more difficult the tasks of achieving justice in this world and leading men to the next. The two theologians agree in many of their judgments concerning certain tendencies in the history of Christian thought. For instance, they rule out the extremist expressions of withdrawal from culture or accomodation to it that punctuate the long history of the Christian faith. Nevertheless, their systems allow for openness to the varied contributions made throughout that history.

Although Maritain takes an analogic or synthetic approach and Niebuhr takes a paradoxic or dualist approach, both can be said to respect the full range of insights represented in the broad tradition of Christian political theology. Indeed, Maritain guards against the natural tendency to err on the side of continuity by constantly emphasizing the ambiguity of the world in relation to Truth. And Niebuhr guards against the natural tendency to err on the side of discontinuity by consistently rejecting the dualistic separation of the two realms. Niebuhr modifies the typical Lutheran approach by reasserting the dynamic interplay between the two authorities, between the sacred and the temporal. On his side, Maritain modifies the typical scholastic approach by reintroducing the note of tension between the two laws, which was obscured by the dazzling vision of a link between the natural and the supernatural.

Thus we see that Maritain's and Niebuhr's approaches represent complementary opposites in political theology. Their emphases regarding the continuity and discontinuity of the spiritual and the temporal are certainly opposed: Maritain underscores the former and Niebuhr the latter. But the nuances of their statements on the two-realms problem reveal a deeper complementarity of approach. Analogy and paradox become, in their hands, opposite sides of the same coin. The same orthodox Christian political theology, cryptically prescribed by Jesus' command regarding Caesar's due and God's due, is encapsulated in two distinct systems. Given these considerations, it may even be possible to view the two-realms problem in alternately optimistic and pessimistic terms—sometimes as analogy, sometimes as paradox—as seems to have been the actual practice of both Maritain and Niebuhr. It is on this basis that we may begin to envision the possibilities of a combined Roman Catholic-Protestant approach to the problem of religion and politics, a truly ecumenical political theology.

TOWARD AN ECUMENICAL POLITICAL THEOLOGY

> To say the least, Roman Catholics and Protestants share
> common questions that provide the agenda for Christian ethics;
> they also share a perplexity about how to answer them, and they
> increasingly share a common set of considerations to be taken
> into account in answering them.
>
> James M. Gustafson
> *Protestant and Roman Catholic Ethics*[1]

---

[1]Subtitled *Prospects for Rapprochement* (Chicago: University of Chicago
Press, 1978) 159.

VI

The political ideals of Jacques Maritain and Reinhold Niebuhr represent distinct yet converging visions of the just society, which can be characterized with the phrase "democratic pluralism and human rights." They each, in their own unique ways, formulate a theology of freedom. This raises the possibility of constructing a genuinely cooperative, ecumenical, Christian political theology.

It may seem, at first glance, that such an endeavor is in danger of falling into the error of providing religious sanctification for a morally ambiguous political movement, democratic pluralism—an error that both Maritain and Niebuhr condemned. After all, democratic pluralism and respect for human rights are rooted in a particular Western cultural tradition. How can democratic pluralism avoid the moral ambiguity that characterizes all historical political systems? How can these themes be universally applied to the divergent strands of world culture? The solution must lie in the fact that it is possible to construct a *théologie politique* which judges the temporal order in light of spiritual values, but which does not become a *politische Theologie* in the service of a "Sacred Empire."[2]

---

[2]Maritain's view of the two types of political theology is discussed at the outset of ch. 1.

Such an ecumenical political theology, based on the work of Maritain, Niebuhr, and others, is possible. Yet we must remember that "democratic pluralism" and "human rights" are mere words, more or less adequate, for describing certain forms of proximate justice that have come closest to fulfilling the ideals of liberty, equality, and fraternity. These ideals, as we have seen, are inherently compatible with the Christian world view.

The writings of Maritain and Niebuhr provide an informed and balanced expression of the classical themes of Christian political theology. To be certain, each thinker gives voice to such expressions in his own distinctive idiom, on the basis of his Roman Catholic or Protestant world view. But they both arrive at quite similar practical conclusions about the characteristics of the free society in the contemporary world. I have compared their interpretative models of practical wisdom and realism. I have surveyed their insights into some of the historical roots of Christian political theology. I have focused attention on their detailed descriptions of the democratic-pluralist society and its mechanisms for defending human rights. And finally, I have explored the question of conceptual styles in approaching the relationship between the two realms of religion and politics, concluding that the approaches of Maritain and Niebuhr are complementary opposites. What do the conclusions of this study imply with regard to hopes for constructing an ecumenical Christian political theology?

"Practical wisdom" and "realism" are the basic interpretative principles of the political theologies of Maritain and Niebuhr, respectively. At the core, both terms signify a political skill, the capacity to understand the social order, to form judgments, and to act—all on the basis of a moral critique of power. Practical wisdom is dedicated to the preservation of the truly human values of truth, human dignity, freedom, and brotherhood that lie at the heart of the gospel ethic. Practical wisdom accepts the fallenness of the world and the intractability of human behavior, as it steadily searches for more complete realizations of the temporal destiny of the human person. Realism, likewise, is dedicated to pursuing a genuinely progressive social ethic that takes account of the drives, interests, and power relationships of actual persons and historical situations. In a number of ways, practical wisdom and realism are tied to the traditional Christian virtues of prudence, justice, courage, and temperance. Prudence, traditionally understood, is the mother of the cardinal virtues, encompassing and balancing each of the others: justice, courage, and temperance.

Maritain sees prudence as the central quality of political leadership, the quality of well-acting that was considered essential in Aristotelian and Thomistic political philosophy. Niebuhr sees the crux of the relation between the two realms as a tension between the virtues of justice and love. Justice is comprised of the regulative concepts of liberty and equality; it is the act of giving each his due, as the ancients understood. Yet, in the Christian world view, justice is transcended and judged by the highest theological virtue, love, which is symbolized by Christ's atonement for sinful humanity. Love offers a perpetual critique of the relative justice that is achieved in this world.

Together, prudence, justice, and love, in tandem with the concepts of practical wisdom and realism, are the fundamental building blocks of an ecumenical Christian political theology. Roman Catholic and Protestant perspectives on social ethics are encapsulated in these rich concepts. Of course, other traditions of Christianity, such as the Eastern Orthodox traditions, should be included in order to achieve a truly ecumenical view. Nevertheless, a synthesis of the themes prominent in the works of Maritain and Niebuhr would constitute a major portion of the work of building a globally Christian political theology.

The second element of an ecumenical political theology would be a substantial consensus regarding the major historical contributions to the Christian view of social justice. The history of Christian and other sources takes shape in the writings of Maritain and Niebuhr as the story of the struggle between two authorities. It is principally a struggle between the claims of the state to absolute allegiance from its subjects and the claims of conscience and the human spirit to certain inalienable rights. The biblical tradition supplies the basic distinction between the things that are Caesar's and the things that are God's. Moses and the Hebrew Prophets appealed to a God whose justice transcends the particular national interests of his chosen people. Jesus' disciples preached with a dedication to the Almighty God who demands a loyalty deeper than political obligation. The Greek and Roman philosophers contributed as well to ancient concepts of justice and right. The theologians of the church, principally Augustine, Aquinas, Luther, and Calvin, added their own distinctive refinements of the doctrine of the two realms. Numerous other theologians, ancient, modern, and contemporary, have made additional contributions to the Christian understanding of politics. Maritain and Niebuhr interpret each of these thinkers and their concepts as essential to the full story of political theology. At times their evaluations of a particular theologian differ; more often they are in agreement. An ecumenical political theology must sort out the elements of this entire tradition, reach a partial consensus, and continue to debate the relevance and appropriateness of some of the component ideas in the tradition. The historical interpretations propounded by Maritain and Niebuhr are an excellent place to begin this debate.

Maritain and Niebuhr describe the democratic-pluralist society as one that is made up of critical and responsible citizens who freely choose to participate in the numerous mediating institutions comprising the body politic. The state is a specialized part of political society; it is charged with certain specific functions but also limited in the range of human action it may legitimately control. The state must respect the inalienable rights of its citizens and be responsive to procedures of popular self-government. The goods of political society that result from such a system—liberty, equality, fraternity—are not mere ideals. They are actual, experienced realities in those nations that have more or less successfully established a democratic pluralist polity that respects human rights.

Probably no more central task awaits the would-be practitioners of an ecumenical political theology than that of thinking clearly about realities. Agreement upon goals and ideals is relatively simple compared to the ambiguous question of interpreting present-day realities, choosing means and paths to greater justice, and ascertaining progress. A clue to the solution of this problem is present in the historically rooted approaches of Maritain and Niebuhr. Neither theologian worships blindly at the altar of Western civilization. Instead, each gives a qualified assent to those tangible experiments in democratic pluralism (now practiced by Eastern as well as Western nations) that have managed to create proximate justice and respect for human rights. Both the theoretical ideals of order and justice, and the practical wisdom of following historical models, are necessary to the formulation of an ecumenical political theology.

Finally, however, it is important to remember that each strand of Christian political thought is distinct and unique. Some have strengths and weaknesses that others may not share. Maritain and Niebuhr represent two conceptual styles of apprehending the relationship of Christ and culture. Niebuhr's style suggests a paradoxic relationship between the eternal and the temporal, just as he postulates a necessary tension between love and justice. Maritain's approach represents an analogic understanding of the relationship between the two realms; he emphasizes the continuity rather than the paradoxic discontinuity between Christ and culture, while he still insists that it is necessary to distinguish between the two realms in order correctly to understand their ultimate unity. A truly ecumenical Christian political theology must incorporate the best ideas from each style of relating Christ and culture. Certain distortions or excesses require correction, but the final ecumenical consensus must affirm each strand of the Christian tradition. The approaches exemplified by Maritain and Niebuhr can be seen as complementary opposites: both are responding to Jesus' enigmatic command to render what is due both to Caesar and to God.

This brief summary illustrates the richness of insights and comparisons resulting from a study of the political theologies of Jacques Maritain and Reinhold Niebuhr. In addition, I have suggested that the complementarity evident in this pair of twentieth-century theologians—one Roman Catholic, the other Protestant—may indicate possibilities for an ecumenical Christian political theology. Such a theology would be a political theology of freedom; that is, it would be based on the ideals of democratic pluralism and human rights, but it would also affirm social experiments that have only partially achieved these ideals in the actual world. If such a consensus were possible among Christians of varying doctrinal persuasions, then the world would be somewhat closer to achieving a global community of interdependent, democratic-pluralist nations that respect and defend fundamental human rights.

APPENDIX

THREE REVIEWS
BY REINHOLD NIEBUHR

[Note: Reproduced below with permission are the texts of three reviews by Reinhold Niebuhr of books by Jacques and Raïssa Maritain. In the case of the first review, Niebuhr was also reviewing a book by Nicholas Berdyaev. No comparisons are drawn between Berdyaev and Jacques Maritain, and their books are treated independently of each other. Only that portion of the review that deals with Maritain is reproduced below. The sources are as follows: Reinhold Niebuhr, "Thomism and Mysticism," review of *Freedom in the Modern World*, by Jacques Maritain, and *Freedom and the Spirit*, by Nicholas Berdyaev, in *Saturday Review*, 8 August 1936, 16; Reinhold Niebuhr, review of *True Humanism*, by Jacques Maritain, in *Radical Religion* 4 (Spring 1939): 45; Reinhold Niebuhr, "Bergson and Maritain," review of *Ransoming the Time*, by Jacques Maritain, and *We Have Been Friends Together*, by Raïssa Maritain, in *Union Seminary Quarterly Review* 3 (March 1942): 28-29.]

Thomism and Mysticism

Maritain is one of a number of French Catholic thinkers who are interpreting the cultural and social crisis in the light of Thomistic theology. While his book hardly compares in solidity of scholarship with the recently published Gifford lectures—"The Spirit of Medieval Philosophy," by Etienne Gilson—its merit lies in his effort to apply Catholic social philosophy to the economic and political problems of our era.

Maritain is more successful in commending a Catholic theistic humanism as a basis for a new world culture than in working out the political and economic details. He properly distinguishes the humanism of Thomistic thought from secular humanism on the one hand and the less humanistic theism of the Protestant Barthian theologians on the other. In terms of such a humanism he is able to escape the individualism of secular liberalism with his emphasis that the good of the community is the highest value "in the scale of terrestrial values." At the same time he avoids the final subordination of the individual to the community as an end in itself by his insistence that the ultimate possibilities of personality transcend the social purposes for which individuals are claimed in their various political and economic collectivities. In elaborating Thomistic social philosophy in terms of this problem he reveals the very great resources of a genuine theistic humanism, which most moderns have ignorantly spurned, and shows how easily a purely secular humanism may become self-devouring.

In his concrete proposals for the building of a new world order under Catholic guidance he is less convincing. He wants neither capitalism nor communism. A type of guild socialism seems to him to conform best to the Christian ideal. But he is as unrealistic as the rationalistic liberals, whose approach he rejects, in explaining how that kind of social order is to be created. He pleads for a priority of politics over economics but does not face the problem that a technical age has made economic power the most basic power, from which political power is derived. In this and in other respects he fails to recognize the dynamic and quasi-autonomous character of the various materials with which a modern statesman must deal. One gains the impression that a Catholicism which once dominated a comparatively static agrarian society will have greater difficulty than it realizes in insinuating its ideals into the dynamic forces of a technical age.

Maritain faces the same difficulties in relating an authoritarian institution to the complexities of a civilization which no longer recognizes a single spiritual authority. The church is to him the instrument of the supremacy of spiritual values over material ones. He does not face the fact that every cultural and spiritual institution is in constant danger of becoming the handmaiden of the dominant forces in society. He neatly dismisses the whole problem of "ideologies" and the religious sanctification of economic interests by admitting the secular influence upon religious ideals only in the decadent period of the Renaissance.

In relating the church to the state he scorns both the secular ideal of tolerance and the old authoritarian ideal of the state as the secular arm of the church. His compromise is full of unconvincing ambiguities. In the same way he does not want Catholic political parties, being particularly critical of the achievements of the Center party of pre-Hitler Germany. He wants Catholics in all political parties and he expects them to guide the policies of these parties in accordance with Catholic presuppositions. There is, in short, not too much clarity in any of his proposals for the detailed problems of the political order.

Review of *True Humanism*

Of all Catholic interpretations of modern ethical and religious problems, that of Maritain, expounded in "True Humanism," would probably come closest to the views generally held by socialist Christians of Protestant persuasion. This is not to say that Maritain is either a socialist or a Christian. But he is a profound Catholic philosopher with a genuine appreciation of the social problem. He is critical of Marxism at precisely the points where we have been critical. He sees that Marxist utopianism is a necessary consequence of its naturalism and materialism. It desires to establish the Kingdom of God in history and thus expects the unconditioned good within the relativities of history. But unlike most Catholic critics of Marxism, he has a genuine understanding of the fateful and necessary role which the workers must play in the reconstruction of society and of the genuine contributions which Marxist philosophy has made to their discovery of that role. His criticism of Barthian theology as "anti-humanist" and a "return to the pure pessimism of primitive Protestantism" will find sympathetic echoes among us, though it must be admitted that the Catholic position will seem, from the Protestant perspective, to err on the other side and to be too uncritical toward the moral realities of the redeemed man in the church.

In his chapters on a new Christian society, Maritain has his greatest difficulty in outlining a plan for a society in which Catholic principles would be the guiding forces of social reconstruction, without making the Catholic church the dominant social authority as in the Middle Ages. Maritain is too much of a realist to regard the latter development as a possibility; and he is not even certain that it would be desirable. But in working out his outline for a future society Catholic authoritarian presuppositions come in conflict with his purpose to maintain a democratic society and it cannot be said that he solves this conflict very satisfactorily.

While the book therefore lacks relevance as far as its plans of construction are concerned, it is one of the ablest analyses of the difference between Christian and modern humanist presuppositions which could be found. It proves conclusively that the Christian faith has unique perspectives upon the nature of man and society which must be set in sharp contrast to modern interpretations, whether liberal or Marxian, no matter how much the modern Christian may profit from these interpretations.

Bergson and Maritain

It is not often that one has the opportunity of reviewing two books by a man and his wife together. During the holidays I had the pleasure of reading Dr. Maritain's *Ransoming the Time* and his wife's autobiography at the same time. But the fact that they were published together would hardly justify a joint review. What does justify it is the significant position which Bergson holds in both books.

A goodly portion of the famous French Catholic philosopher's book is devoted to the exposition of the Christian conception of time and eternity in contrast to Bergson's, which Dr. Maritain quite rightly regards as a half-way house to Christianity. Bergson understands the significance of time and the importance of history, as Christianity does; but unlike Christianity he seeks to comprehend the whole of reality within the concept, or rather the experience of, duration. Maritain appreciates Bergson's fear of conceptualizing what transcends time. But he also proves that duration is an inadequate category of ultimate reality, that life cannot be understood except from the standpoint of the divine reality which transcends the flux of time.

Maritain's appreciation of and polemic against Bergson is set in an interesting light by his wife's autobiography, which is of course also to a considerable degree a biography of Maritain. Madame Maritain reveals to what degree Bergson was to them a halfway house to the Christian faith historically as well as logically; how eagerly they went to his lectures and found a new light there which saved them from the despair to which they were tempted by the arid rationalism and relativism of the intellectual circles in which they moved. Madame Maritain reports that, once they had decided to become Catholics they went through a period of spiritual "dryness" which their spiritual advisors promised would end with their baptism. They were assailed by doubts of al kinds. Being socially minded, they were embarrassed by the hiatus between Christianity as a faith and the lack of social awareness in the actual historical church. The promise of their advisors was fulfilled and with their baptism came a serenity of faith which has never left them. Madame Maritain attributes this to the efficacy of sacramental grace, though a Protestant might insist that it proves the truth of the words of St. Augustine that there are some things which must be believed in order to be understood, which is to say that no amount of intellectual preparation can finally supply the link between the soul and God in faith. The sacrament may well be helpful in this venture of faith, though a Protestant would not make faith as directly dependent upon the sacrament. Be that as it may, the spiritual insights derived from the pilgrimage of these two sincere and profound souls, are rewarding indeed.

Dr. Maritain's book is of course devoted to many other subjects beside the primary one of the Christian conception of time and eternity. There is an interesting chapter on the Jews, on which subject Dr. Maritain writes more movingly than any other Christian theologian, private experience and religious faith combining to give his words a special poignancy and profundity. His chapter on Pascal will be of particular interest to Protestants because every criticism which Maritain makes of Pascal could of course be made against Protestantism itself. This essay reveals to what degree Pascal was really a Reformation theologian in the heart of the church. Some of Maritain's criticisms, particularly those in which

he insists that Pascal's pessimism betrayed him into a defeatist attitude toward the problem of justice, could be made with equal
relevance against modern forms of radical Reformation theology.

SELECTED BIBLIOGRAPHY

[*Note:* The most complete bibliography of the works of Reinhold Niebuhr is D. B. Robertson, ed., *Reinhold Niebuhr's Works: A Bibliography* (Boston: G. K. Hall & Co., 1979). Currently being prepared under the auspices of the International Jacques Maritain Institute are *The Complete Works of Jacques and Raïssa Maritain* and a bibliographic index of the written works on the life and thought of Jacques and Raïssa Maritain. In the meantime one should consult Donald and Idella Gallagher, *The Achievement of Jacques and Raïssa Maritain: A Bibliography 1906-1961* (Garden City NY: Doubleday & Co., 1962); and Joseph W. Evans, "A Maritain Bibliography," *New Scholasticism* 46 (1972): 118-28. The following list includes the works of Niebuhr and Maritain, as well as selected additional sources that have been cited in the present study. Only the English translations of a number of Maritain's books are listed; in each case there is reasonable certainty as to the accuracy of the translation.]

Books

Ahn, Chee Soon. "A Comparative Study of the Political Ideas of Two Contemporary Theologians: Reinhold Niebuhr and Jacques Maritain." Dissertation, Florida State University, 1966.

Amato, Joseph. *Mounier and Maritain: A French Catholic Understanding of the Modern World.* University AL: University of Alabama Press, 1975.

Aquinas, Thomas. *On Charity.* Translated by Lottie H. Kendzierski. Medieval Philosophical Texts in Translation, no. 10. Milwaukee: Marquette University Press, 1960.

Aristotle. *Nicomachean Ethics.* Translated by Martin Ostwald. Indianapolis: Bobbs-Merrill, Library of Liberal Arts, 1962.

Berger, Peter L., and Richard John Neuhaus. *To Empower People: The Role of Mediating Structures in Public Policy.* Washington, D.C.: American Enterprise Institute for Public Policy Research, 1977.

Bluhm, William T. *Theories of the Political System: Classics of Political Thought and Modern Political Analysis.* Englewood Cliffs NJ: Prentice-Hall, 1965.

Bonhoeffer, Dietrich. *Ethics.* Edited by Eberhard Bethge. Translated by Neville Horton Smith. New York: Macmillan Co., 1955.

Chesterton, G. K. *Saint Thomas Aquinas.* London: Sheed & Ward, 1933; reprint, Garden City NY: Doubleday & Co., Image Books, 1956.

d'Entreves, Alexander Passerin. *The Medieval Contribution to Political Thought: Thomas Aquinas, Marsilius of Padua, Richard Hooker.* Oxford: Oxford University Press, 1939; reprint, New York: Humanities Press, 1959.

Erikson, Erik H. *Gandhi's Truth: On the Origins of Militant Nonviolence.* New York: W. W. Norton & Co., 1969.

Frankel, Charles. *The Case for Modern Man.* New York: Harper & Bros., 1955.

Fuchs, Joseph. *Natural Law: A Theological Investigation.* Translated by Helmut Reckter and John A. Dowling. New York: Sheed & Ward, 1965.

Gustafson, James M. *Protestant and Roman Catholic Ethics: Prospects for Rapprochement.* Chicago: University of Chicago Press, 1978.

Landon, Harold R., ed. *Reinhold Niebuhr: A Prophetic Voice in Our Time.* Greenwich CT: Seabury Press, 1962.

Lippmann, Walter. *U.S. Foreign Policy: Shield of the Republic.* Boston: Little, Brown & Co., Atlantic Monthly Press, 1943.

Lonergan, Bernard J. F. *Insight: A Study of Human Understanding.* London: Longmans, Green & Co., 1958; reprint, New York: Harper & Row, 1978.

Longwood, Walter M. "The Ends of Government in the Thought of Reinhold Niebuhr and Jacques Maritain: A Study in Christian Social Ethics." Dissertation, Yale University, 1969.

Maritain, Jacques. *Carnet de Notes.* Paris: Desclée de Brouwer, 1965.

_____. *Christianity and Democracy.* Translated by Doris C. Anson. New York: Charles Scribner's Sons, 1944.

_____. *Freedom in the Modern World.* Translated by Richard O'Sullivan. New York: Charles Scribner's Sons, 1936; reprint, New York: Gordian Press, 1971.

_____. *Integral Humanism: Temporal and Spiritual Problems of a New Christendom.* Translated by Joseph W. Evans. New York: Charles Scribner's Sons, 1968; reprint, Notre Dame IN: University of Notre Dame Press, 1973.

_____. *Man and the State.* Chicago: University of Chicago Press, Phoenix Books, 1951.

_____. *The Peasant of the Garonne: An Old Layman Questions Himself about the Present Time.* Translated by Michael Cuddihy and Elizabeth Hughes. New York: Holt, Rinehart & Winston, 1968; reprint, New York: Macmillan Co., 1969.

_____. *The Person and the Common Good.* Translated by John J. Fitzgerald. New York: Charles Scribner's Sons, 1947; reprint, Notre Dame IN: University of Notre Dame Press, 1966.

_____. *Reflections on America.* New York: Charles Scribner's Sons, 1958; reprint, New York: Gordian Press, 1975.

_____. *The Rights of Man and Natural Law.* Translated by Doris C. Anson. New York: Charles Scribner's Sons, 1943; reprint, New York: Gordian Press, 1971.

_____. *The Social and Political Philosophy of Jacques Maritain: Selected Readings.* Edited by Joseph W. Evans and Leo R. Ward. New York: Charles Scribner's Sons, 1955; reprint, Notre Dame IN: University of Notre Dame Press, 1976.

_____. *The Things That Are Not Caesar's.* Translated by J. F. Scanlan. London: Sheed & Ward, 1930.

_____. *Trois Réformateurs.* Paris: Librairie Plon, 1925.

Murray, John Courtney. *We Hold These Truths: Catholic Reflections on the American Proposition.* New York: Sheed & Ward, 1960; reprint, Garden City NY: Doubleday & Co., Image Books, 1964.

Niebuhr, H. Richard. *Christ and Culture.* New York: Harper & Row, Harper Torchbooks, 1956.

Niebuhr, Reinhold. *Beyond Tragedy: Essays on the Christian Interpretation of History.* New York: Charles Scribner's Sons, Scribner Library, 1937.

_____. *The Children of Light and the Children of Darkness: A Vindication of Democracy and a Critique of Its Traditional Defense.* New York: Charles Scribner's Sons, Scribner Library, 1944.

_____. *Christian Realism and Political Problems.* New York: Charles Scribner's Sons, 1953; reprint, Fairfield NJ: Augustus M. Kelley, 1977.

_____. *Christianity and Power Politics.* New York: Charles Scribner's Sons, 1940; reprint, Hamden CT: Archon Books, 1969.

_____. *Faith and History: A Comparison of Christian and Modern Views of History.* New York: Charles Scribner's Sons, 1949.

_____. *Faith and Politics: A Commentary on Religious, Social and Political Thought in a Technological Age.* Edited by Ronald H. Stone. New York: George Braziller, 1968.

_____. *An Interpretation of Christian Ethics.* New York: Harper & Bros., 1935; reprint, New York: Meridian Books, Living Age Books, 1956.

_____. *Love and Justice: Selections from the Shorter Writings of Reinhold Niebuhr.* Edited by D. B. Robertson. Philadelphia: Westminster Press, 1957; reprint, Gloucester MA: Peter Smith, 1976.

_____. *Man's Nature and His Communities: Essays on the Dynamics and Enigmas of Man's Personal and Social Existence.* New York: Charles Scribner's Sons, 1965.

_____. *Moral Man and Immoral Society: A Study in Ethics and Politics.* New York: Charles Scribner's Sons, Scribner Library, 1973.

_____. *The Nature and Destiny of Man.* 2 vols. New York: Charles Scribner's Sons, Scribner Library, 1941-1943.

_____. *Pious and Secular America.* New York: Charles Scribner's Sons, 1958; reprint, Fairfield NJ: Augustus M. Kelley, 1977.

_____. *Reflections on the End of an Era.* New York: Charles Scribner's Sons, 1934.

_____. *Reinhold Niebuhr on Politics: His Political Philosophy and Its Application to Our Age as Expressed in His Writings.* Edited by Harry R. Davis and Robert C. Good. New York: Charles Scribner's Sons, 1960.

_____. *The Self and the Dramas of History.* New York: Charles Scribner's Sons, 1955.

_____. *The Structure of Nations and Empires: A Study of the Recurring Patterns and Problems of the Political Order in Relation to the Unique Problems of the Nuclear Age.* New York: Charles Scribner's Sons, 1959; reprint, Fairfield NJ: Augustus M. Kelley, 1977.

Niebuhr, Reinhold, and Paul E. Sigmund. *The Democratic Experience: Past and Prospects.* New York: Frederick A. Praeger, 1969.

Nottingham, William J. *Christian Faith and Secular Action.* St. Louis: Bethany Press, 1968.

Novak, Michael. *The Spirit of Democratic Capitalism*. New York: Simon & Schuster, 1982.

Peardon, Thomas P., Introduction to *The Second Treatise of Government*, by John Locke. Edited by Thomas P. Peardon. Indianapolis: Bobbs-Merrill, Library of Liberal Arts, 1952.

Pieper, Josef. *The Four Cardinal Virtues: Prudence, Justice, Fortitude, Temperance*. Notre Dame IN: University of Notre Dame Press, 1966.

Ramsey, Paul. *Nine Modern Moralists*. Englewood Cliffs NJ: Prentice-Hall, 1962; reprint, New York: New American Library, Mentor Books, 1970.

Reveley, Walter T. "A Christian Critique of Modern Liberal Democratic Theory as Reflected in the Writings of Jacques Maritain, A. D. Lindsay and Reinhold Niebuhr." Dissertation, Duke University, 1953.

Ross, W. D. *Aristotle: A Complete Exposition of His Works and Thought*. 5th rev. ed. New York: World Publishing Co., 1959.

Sanders, Thomas G. *Protestant Concepts of Church and State: Historical Backgrounds and Approaches for the Future*. New York: Holt, Rinehart & Winston, 1964; reprint, Garden City NY: Doubleday & Co., Anchor Books, 1965.

Articles

Germino, Dante L. "Two Types of Recent Christian Political Thought." *The Journal of Politics* 21 (August 1959): 455-86.

Hutchinson, Roger C. "Reinhold Niebuhr and 'Contextual Connections.' " Response by John H. Berthong. *This World*, no. 6 (Fall 1983): 102-14.

McCann, Dennis. "Reinhold Niebuhr and Jacques Maritain on Marxism: A Comparison of Two Traditional Models of Practical Theology." *Journal of Religion* 58 (April 1978): 140-68.

Niebuhr, Reinhold. "After Capitalism—What?" *The World Tomorrow* 16 (1 March 1933): 203-205.

_____. "The Anomaly of European Socialism." *The Yale Review* 42 (December 1952): 161-67.

_____. "Bergson and Maritain." Review of *Ransoming the Time*, by Jacques Maritain, and *We Have been Friends Together*, by Raïssa Maritain. *Union Seminary Quarterly Review* 3 (March 1942): 28-29.

_____. "Biblical Faith and Socialism: A Critical Appraisal." In *Religion and Culture: Essays in Honor of Paul Tillich*, 44-57. Edited by Walter Leibrecht. New York: Harper & Bros., 1959.

_____. "The Creed of Modern Christian Socialists." *Radical Religion* 3 (Spring 1938): 13-18.

_____. "The Death of the President." *Christianity and Crisis* 5 (30 April 1945): 4-6.

_____. "Education and the World Scene." *Daedalus* 88 (Winter 1959): 107-20.

_____. "A Fourth Term for Roosevelt." *The New Statesman and Nation* 25 (15 May 1943): 315-16.

_____. "Frontier Fellowship." *Christianity and Society* 13 (Autumn 1948): 3.

_____. "Notes." *Christianity and Society* 8 (Spring 1943): 11.

_____. "A Reorientation of Radicalism." *The World Tomorrow* 16 (July 1933): 443-44.

_____. Review of *True Humanism*, by Jacques Maritain. *Radical Religion* 4 (Spring 1939): 45.

_____. "Thomism and Mysticism." Review of *Freedom in the Modern World*, by Jacques Maritain, and *Freedom and the Spirit*, by Nicholas Berdyaev. *Saturday Review*, 8 August 1936, 16.

_____. "The World Council of Churches." *Christianity and Society* 13 (Autumn 1948): 3-5.

INDEX